Sacred Sites of the West

Sacred Sites of the West
A Guide to Mystical Centers

Edited by Frank Joseph

ISBN 0-88839-404-7
Copyright © 1997 Frank Joseph

Canadian Cataloguing in Publication Data

Main entry under title:
Sacred sites of the west

Includes bibliographical references.
ISBN 0-88839-404-7

1. Sacred space—West (U.S.)—Guidebooks. 2. Sacred
space—Canada, Western—Guidebooks. 3. West
(U.S.)—Guidebooks. 4. Canada, Western—Guidebooks. I.
Joseph, Frank.
F590.3.S32 1997   291.3'5'0978   C97-910099-2

Printed in Hong Kong by Colorcraft

Editor: Nancy Miller
Production/Cover Design: Andrew Jaster

Published simultaneously in Canada and the United States by

HANCOCK HOUSE PUBLISHERS LTD.
19313 Zero Avenue, Surrey, BC V4P 1M7
(604) 538-1114 Fax (604) 538-2262

HANCOCK HOUSE PUBLISHERS
1431 Harrison Avenue, Blaine, WA 98230-5005
(604) 538-1114 Fax (604) 538-2262

Dedication

To my mother, Virginia, who gave new life to "sacred sites."

Contents

Introduction

The Great Pyramid of Egypt. Britain's Stonehenge. The Acropolis at Athens. These are the places people generally think of when "sacred sites" are mentioned. But it is not necessary to travel overseas or to only the most famous sites for a personal, mystical experience at a spiritually charged spot of deep antiquity.

Unknown to most North Americans, this land has its own prehistoric pyramids, as well as a full-scale replica of Stonehenge, not in ruins, but as it appeared when new. Beyond these unsuspected parallels with the Old World, North America abounds with natural and man-made locations of unique and profound spiritual powers. Largely unrecognized, sacred sites occur throughout North America, sometimes in our own backyards. The purpose of this guidebook is to acquaint readers with these domestic sites in the West; to define their numinous qualities and help readers tap into their special energies.

There are growing numbers of books about sacred centers on the market. *Sacred Sites of the West* stands out from the rest in that it covers the spiritual as well as the physical aspects of many magical sites unknown even to adepts on the subject. Many guides to mystical centers are written by persons who have never even seen the places they presume to know; their descriptions are often replete with misleading information. Contrary to the remote speculations of these armchair authors, all the contributors to this guidebook describe sacred centers that are intimately known to them, sites which are often near their homes and with which they have been personally acquainted for many years.

But what exactly is a sacred site? It is a place of singular numinous (mystical) power generated by focused spiritual forces. Sometimes known as "vortexes," sacred sites are concentrated points of psychic or soul energy put there by cosmic and natural forces of Earth and sky or caused by the interaction of human awareness and the eternal vitalities of Nature which still resonate at the site, long after the person has departed. Some places belong to ancient civilizations, while others echo with the spiritual vibrations of more historical, even contemporary, human actions. Still other centers are pure manifestations of the soul of Nature, the immortal gods or the Great Spirit. We feel drawn into these sometimes dimly familiar Otherworlds to partake of their variety of magic and recharge our spiritual batteries; to heal the Earth and to allow Mother Earth to heal us; to find answers to questions from an alternative, higher or deeper reality; to reassure ourselves of our own significance in the grand scheme of eternity; to feel our roots in Nature and the past; to trace the fabric of Destiny. As such, visitors to sacred centers are not mere tourists, but pilgrims on a very personal quest for enlightenment and empowerment.

Few persons who seek out the places described in *Sacred Sites of the West* will fail to be mightily impressed by their mystery and beauty. Indeed, a sense of wonder is essential to a full-bodied appreciation of any sacred area. But our higher purpose should be to communicate with a site, if not in words, then in emotion. To experience such a special place with a detached and analytical attitude may have its rewards, although a soul-to-soul contact with the resident *genii* can be more personally significant. There is no revelation without correct and willing openness.

The individual pilgrim should come to a sacred center with humble reverence and a pure heart. Nothing specific should be expected or antici-pated, thus leaving ourselves open to whatever the site wishes to offer us. If we do not always receive what we desire, we are almost invariably presented with something we need. We must approach the *genius loci*, the spirit of the place, with veneration and a sense of giving. Gladly we take whatever the site has to offer, and are sincerely grateful for the opportu-nity to visit. Only in such a respectful mindset will sacred centers live for us. If we make ourselves worthy of their interest, they will miraculously reveal themselves to us.

It is important, too, to leave something of ourselves behind in holy places. A pinched offering of tobacco or sage, a few drops of blessed or pure water, a seed or flower from your garden, a crystal or attractive stone; gifts such as these are appropriate and powerful. They go on working long after the visit has ended, serving as links between the pilgrim and the sacred place.

Certainly, the ideal medium for accessing a spiritually charged site is meditation, either before or after, but especially during a visit. Meditation clears the mind and opens our inner awareness to the voices, music and visions of a sacred center. Readers unfamiliar with simple meditation techniques are urged to read *Meditation, the Inner Way* by Naomi Hum-phrey (Aquarian Press, Thorsons Publishing Group, Wellingborough, Northhampshire NN8 2RQ, England, 1987). Humphrey's straightforward explanations and effective methods may be mastered with little time and effort.

A common form of meditation useful at most sacred centers involves controlled breathing. Sit comfortably in a quiet place, eyes closed. Take a deep breath through the nostrils, hold it for seven counts, then exhale out the mouth as though blowing out a candle flame. Repeat twice more. Then breathe normally, counting each inhalation. At the forty-second breath, count the inhalations back down to one. For the duration, concentrate only on breathing and counting. Mental disturbances, outside sounds and stray thoughts are normal and do not invalidate the entire meditation. Ignore them, let them pass and complete the count. Finish by taking three deep breaths as at the beginning. The numbers involved in this method are very old and sacred. Seven is the number signifying the completion of cycles, while three is universally associated with Divinity. Forty-two represents six sets of seven, six being the number of Perfection. Over the Ancient Egyptian Otherworld presided the forty-two Judges, symbolizing the attainment of heaven. The sacred numerals implicit in breath meditation are essential to achieving mental clarity through a reoriented balance with the inner order of the cosmos.

Pure meditation, in which the conscious mind is focused on the breathing alone, is certainly appropriate for accessing the resident energies of any sacred center. An alternative, although not necessarily superior form is visualization. As one enters deepening levels of meditation, a conscious effort is made to picture in the imagination a simple, appropriate image or symbol. The advantage of visualization lies in the creation of a powerful, direct link with the "spirit of place." While focusing on a particularly relevant image, the innermost feelings and receptivities of a visitor are often more readily and strongly activated. During both visualization and breathing meditation either the *genius loci*'s own symbolic manifestation or the entity itself may appear in the mind. Such appearances can be startling, to say the least. But visitors are reminded that they are in control at all times and must decide for themselves whether to dwell on the intrusive image or voice, or merely relegate it to part of the meditation. Each pilgrim visiting a sacred center should have no difficulty selecting the proper image on which to concentrate and hold in the mind while meditating.

That the *genius loci* of sacred sites addresses itself to the receptive visitor, there is no doubt. Anecdotes of genuine mystical encounters at these hallowed places are many and convincing.

A valuable aid to highlighting that receptivity and the opening of our inner awareness is the portable tape player. Preselected music appropriate to the character of a particular site, when played while visiting a sacred center, can make the location come alive. It will be found that the music soon becomes something more significant than mere background accompaniment, as it begins to thematically define subtle nuances in the special environment. If the experience has been particularly meaningful, listeners will find that the music selected for their visit will thereafter always evoke that place and its identifiable feelings. There is a wide selection of atmospheric New Age audiotapes from which to choose. Some classical pieces conjure the emotions no less effectively. For example, climbing Alaska's Mt. Denali to the evocative sound of Alan Hovannes's *Magic Mountain Symphony* can be a never-to-be-forgotten event. At other sacred centers Native American dances would seem particularly powerful in helping to visualize the inherent imagery of a site. Music, too, is a gift to the *genius loci*, creating an instant, vibrant bond between the visitor and the visited.

It should be remembered, however, that music is an audio aid, and not always necessary or even appropriate. The pilgrim will often do better by listening to the special sounds of a place, particularly its silences, with the unassisted ear. The visitor must decide what can best assist in the appreciation of each sacred center.

A useful item in the pilgrim's travel kit is a quartz crystal. The numinous qualities of this mineral are clearly introduced by Phyllis Galde in *Crystal Healing, the Next Step* (St. Paul, MN, Llewellyn Publications, 1988). Readers unfamiliar with the mystical properties of crystals are urged to acquaint themselves with her eminently informative investigation. Suffice it to mention here that crystals magnify and store certain forms of energy. They simultaneously enhance the visitor's receptivity and his or her projected spiritual powers. When walking through a sacred center, carry a crystal in the left or receiving hand.

Some of the contributors to *Sacred Sites of the West* were initially reluctant to write publicly of these holy, often vulnerable places. Indeed, a great many spiritual centers are so fragile, our first impulse was to protect them against disclosure. But we have hopefully entered a new age, a chief goal of which is to make spiritually valid phenomena and information available to the curious and the uninitiated. The sacred centers of the Earth were not given exclusively to a secret elite. Rather, they belong to everyone, even at the risk of desecration. We are convinced that this guidebook will do far more good than harm, for the awakening of humankind will not be possible without the personal mystical experiences provided by the hallowed corners of the planet. Moreover, by calling attention to so many hitherto neglected sacred centers, we are lending impetus to their protection under responsible local authorities.

The fundamental responsibility of anyone visiting a sacred spot is to preserve it. Karmic justice awaits persons who willfully damage or desecrate consecrated ground, and simple recognition of this higher law should be sufficient to instill the properly awed respect due in the presence of a holy precinct. Our readers are advised to obey the public authorities entrusted with the maintenance of lands on which hallowed places are located for future generations. Most of the sites described here are already protected by official state agencies.

The great benefit in visiting a sacred center is the deeply personal, mystical experience such a place commands. The mystery religions of the Ancient World flourished for thousands of years because they similarly involved each individual initiate in an intimate communication with Divinity. By meeting with such emotionally transfiguring spiritual forces, we are rendered capable of that which the Greeks called *katharsis*, a "purging" of the human spirit when touched by the Divine and supercharged with profound emotion. Only at such moments are mortals convinced of the reality of their own souls, because they *feel* them. It is precisely this cathartic experience, our link with spiritual reality, that is missing from modern civilization.

Millions of individuals, dissatisfied with the ideals promulgated by our consumer society, are feeling a growing uncertainty, restlessness and inner yearning for higher meaning and greater significance in their lives. They need to go to some special place, some genuine source of spiritual replenishment, to revive their thirsty souls. The sacred centers included here abundantly fill that need. North America is greatly blessed with a large number of these powerful places. And we shall all be richer for seeking them out in our own quest through life.

Frank Joseph,
January 1997

The Writers

D. J. Conway—Author of *Norse Magic* and *Celtic Magic* (Llewellyn, 1988), D. J. is presently working on a book detailing ancient magical practices around the world. She was born and reared in the Columbia Gorge area of Oregon, where her affinity for the state's sacred centers is rooted in her childhood origins.

Lynne Crowe—Lynne was trained as a child by Montana's Salish Indian elders, who had adopted her father. In 1974, she won first place in Llewellyn Publications's *Gnostica Challenge* essay competition, and she has subsequently written for the company's *Gnostica News* and *Moon Sign Book*. After completing her master's degree in linguistic anthropology, she went on to become a nationally recognized teacher of esoterica.

L. Christine Hayes—Born in Venezuela, Christine established the Star of Isis Foundation, a mystery school designed for the enlightenment of human-planetary consciousness through the alchemy of divine origins. She authored *Magii from the Blue Star* (Burning Bush Publications) and the acclaimed *Temple Doors*.

Frank Joseph—A native Chicagoan, Frank is the author of *The Destruction of Atlantis* (Atlantis Research Publishers, 1987), *The Lost Pyramids of Rock Lake* (Galde Press, Inc., 1992) and *Atlantis in Wisconsin* (Galde Press, 1995). He is editor-in-chief of *The Ancient American*, a national magazine describing the impact of overseas visitors on America before the arrival of Columbus.

Anodea Judith—Together with her husband, Richard Ely (a consulting geologist whose photographs accompany his wife's writing), Anodea conducts Science and Mystery Tours to sacred centers, such as Machu Picchu, in Peru. Author of *Wheels of Life: A User's Guide to the Chakra System* (Llewellyn Publications), she is a practicing therapist and teacher of ancient religious beliefs.

LaVedi R. Lafferty—*The Eternal Dance* (Llewellyn Publications, 1984) was an outgrowth of LaVedi's twenty years' teaching experience and her foundation/management of an esoteric center in Alaska. Listed in *Who's Who in the West* and *Foremost Women of the 20th Century*, her expertise extends to meditation techniques, astrology and past-life recall.

Florence McClain—Classical pianist, artist, historian, photographer and archaeologist, her authoritative opinions are regularly sought after for identification of pre-Columbian remains throughout America's Southwest. Florence authored *A Practical Guide to Past-Life Regression* (Llewellyn Publications, 1989), and conducts intensive research into the problem-solving aspects of past-life therapy.

Sandra Rachlis—With degrees in anthropology and sociology, Sandra has insights into Montana's sacred centers that are profound. A psychic and visionary since childhood, she works in close cooperation with the natural and human communities through group ritual, art and hands-on procedures which are methods that bring her in personal contact with the physical elements of a sacred site. These include interpreting the sacred character of a particular landscape or the touching of a stone or mound to open intuitive receptivity.

Glossary

Astral plane—A transconscious level of being, a plane of existence the soul attains beyond the physical body it otherwise inhabits.

Chthonian realm—From Greek mythology, the transmaterial abode of those spirits, helpful or hostile to mankind, dwelling in the Earth.

Deva—A luminous being, from the Sanskrit root *div*, "to shine." Traditionally associated with tree spirits or the nonhuman protectors of Nature, devas are manifestations of animate and inanimate objects, the Soul of Things, inhabiting plants as well as stones, often perceived as personal guides to finding one's path through life.

Ecumene—Greek for a "world community," and referring to a former Golden Age, before the Great Flood, when mankind achieved the first international civilization based not primarily on political, economic or military (i.e., material) values, but foremostly through a unified belief in the eternal nature of the universe, as symbolized in solar worship. Hence, this Golden Age did not refer to mineral wealth, but the gold of sunlight and the immortal principle it signified.

Eleusian mysteries—Called "mysteries" because they were hidden from persons not initiated into the sacred ceremonies and tenets of a cult centered at Eleusis, not far from Athens, in Ancient Greece. The Eleusian mysteries equated human birth, life, death and rebirth with the cycles of Nature, as epitomized in the myth of the Earth Mother, Demeter, and her daughter, Persephone, personification of spring and the eternally renewing principle of the universe.

Genii—Plural of genius, here meant to indicate more than one "spirit of place," or *genius loci*.

Genius loci—Greek for "the spirit of the place."

Geomancy—From the Latin *geo* (Earth) and *mans* (to calculate), an ancient system of wisdom and social application founded on perception of the sacred character of a particular landscape.

Higher and lower energies—Powerful inner transformational human forces with ultimately divine potential for, respectively, creative or destructive purposes. Neither one nor the other is "good" or "bad," save in the moral context of its application.

15

Intaglio—An art work sculpted to form a depression, usually in a stone or the surface of the Earth.

Mandala—Sanskrit for "circular design," a device used to still the observer's thoughts, focusing attention toward a point of deep, inner calm, from which a spiritual quest may be launched or receptivity opened for significant insight. The designs of a mandala are often symbols from what C. G. Jung termed "the collective unconscious," or archetypes, belonging in common to all mankind.

Manitou—Among the Algonquian Indians of North America, a nature-spirit or deity of great spiritual power.

Otherworld—Realms of the soul beyond the human body in which it otherwise dwells. They coexist with our physical dimension and mingle both spiritual and material qualities. Receptive persons may experience these "worlds" at a sacred site—a real location in the physical sense, yet merging elements from another plane of existence.

Oversoul—The Universal Self, the merging of individual human consciousness with the Great Mystery of the Universe, that superconsciousness underlying all Nature, which unifies it and gives it purpose, and from which we experience a sense of oneness with everything in existence.

Planetary energy—Those forces, more personally experienced than scientifically understood, in the Earth which interface with the biocircuity of the human brain to effect an individual connection to the spiritual underpinnings of Nature.

Scry—To prognosticate or achieve altered states of consciousness through meditation on a clear object, such as a quartz crystal or the surface of a calm body of water.

Shaman—From the Russian Tungusic dialect for a spiritual leader who communicates through personal experience with the numinous dimensions of life. In essence, a psychic whose insights are accepted as guidance by the community he or she serves.

Telluric energy—Forces within the Earth which link all living things into the common scheme or superconsciousness of Nature and often spark human transformational experiences. Part of the definition of a "sacred site" is a location at which telluric energies are concentrated and especially in evidence.

Underworld—Sometimes used as another expression for the Otherworld, that dimension beyond the material, but often meant to identify the unseen realm of spiritual forces underlaying the Natural World, particularly as personified in plant and animal spirits, esoterically known as "familiars."

Vision quest—To seek self knowledge, spiritual empowerment and one's true path in life by going to a sacred site or passing through a transformational experience of some kind.

Volcanic breccia—Rocks composed of angular fragments melded together with older rocks through the action of volcanic magma.

Alaska

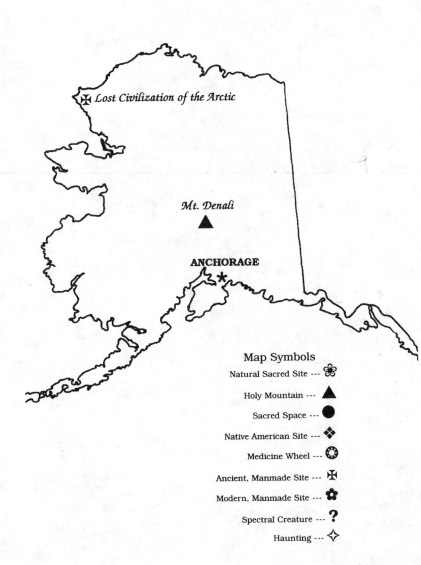

⊞ *Lost Civilization of the Arctic*

Mt. Denali
▲

ANCHORAGE
✳

Map Symbols

Natural Sacred Site --- ✿

Holy Mountain --- ▲

Sacred Space --- ●

Native American Site --- ❖

Medicine Wheel --- ◎

Ancient, Manmade Site --- ⊞

Modern, Manmade Site --- ✿

Spectral Creature --- ?

Haunting --- ◇

Denali
LaVedi R. Lafferty

Mount McKinley, towering above the impressive snow-capped 600-mile (967 km) arc of the Alaska Range at 20,320 feet (6,773 m), is the highest mountain in North America. Measured from the 2,000-foot (667 m) lowlands near Wonder Lake to its summit, its vertical relief of 18,000 feet (6,000 m) (greater than that of Mount Everest) makes it the tallest mountain in the world. Frequently hidden in clouds, the mountain makes its own weather, with permanent snowfields covering over half of its slopes. Ice on the mountain is hundreds of feet thick in places and winter temperatures can plunge to below -75°F (-50°C).

Mount McKinley National Park was established through the efforts of naturalist Charles Sheldon in 1917, who wanted to protect the area's large animal population of moose, caribou, bears, ball sheep (wild sheep named for the clumps of wool which they produce, a unique breed found almost exclusively in this part of the world) and other wildlife. He had wanted the park to be named Denali after the Athabascan name for the mountain, meaning "the high one"; however, his suggestion was not acted upon until 1980. At that time the park boundaries were greatly expanded to include the entire Mount McKinley massif, which more than tripled the size of the park.

The park is now known as Denali National Park and Preserve, though the name of the mountain was not officially changed. Due to the area's significance as a subarctic ecosystem, it is also designated as an International Biosphere Reserve. The park now encompasses 6 million acres (about 1.5 million hectares). The mountain itself is part of the Alaska Range, which divides the interior plateau from south-central Alaska. This range began its formation some 65 million years ago, resulting from the Denali fault, which produced North America's largest crystal break. Two tectonic plates move against each other for 1,300 miles (2,049 km), from the Yukon border to the Aleutian peninsula. Volcanic eruptions are common on the peninsula and earthquake tremors frequently occur in the environs of the park.

The mountain, visible for hundreds of miles in many directions, sits like a crown upon Alaska, The Great Land (an appropriate title derived from the Native name for the country). For untold centuries nomadic people hunted upon Denali's northern reaches, fished the rivers for salmon and gathered edible plants and berries. The summer's harvest was mostly dried in preparation for wintering in warmer areas. Denali remains a largely unspoiled wilderness of wildlife, tundra carpeted with miniaturized plants and flowers, wide valleys with wandering rivers, visible creeping glaciers and panoramic, sweeping vistas.

Mystical Significance

Among the Athabascan Natives, also known as the Tena, ancient tales of creation and magic were transmitted orally, handed down from generation to generation. Since the Tena share a common ancestry with the southern tribes of Navajo and Apache, whose language comes from the same lingual roots, parallels may be expected in their shamanistic traditions. The Alaskan Tena have historically been a peaceful people, following the example of Yako, the ancient shamanistic Adam of their forefathers.

The narrative of Mount Denali's creation was recorded in 1903 by circuit court judge, the Hon. James Wickersham, who had received the story from Koonah, the blind sage and chief of a Tena band. At his seasonal encampment in Kantishna, facing south toward the great mountain, Koonah tells of the divinities and demons associated with Denali. Softly, Koonah speaks of the time long ago, before Denali, the High One, existed. Consistent with other Native traditions, he tells of "the world before," the one that existed before the world as we know it today. He speaks of the battle between good and evil that resulted in the manifestation of our physical world, the creation of a spiritual pantheon and of human procreation.

The old chief continues the tale, describing the magician Yako as straight and tall as a spruce tree, as gentle as a young caribou, as strong as a bull moose and as wise as a beaver. He lives alone, because there are no women in the land, no villages or other people. A mighty shaman, Yako is characterized as having the ability to move with the silence of a shadow and the power to change the form of animals, land and sea; but he desires a wife and has none. Yako is told by Ses, the great brown bear, that far to the west in the village of Totson, the Raven war chief, there are beautiful women of Yako's race. Totson, however, is a mighty hunter of both bear and walrus, and he is a killer of men. This greatly disturbs Yako, until Ses tells him that the women of Totson's village are distressed by bloodshed and death. Yako decides that he will travel to Yunana, the distant sunset land far to the west, to seek a wife from Totson's village.

In the spring, after the winter snows melt, he builds a canoe from spruce and birch wood, covering it with sheets of birch bark sewn with spruce roots and caulked with spruce gum. He launches it upon the mighty Yukon River and drifts upon the current, until he reaches the salt water of the ocean. Yako paddles his canoe across the open waters to the land of Totson. Upon arriving at the seashore of the village, he sings a beautiful song to the Raven chief, describing the land he comes from and his mission. He begs Totson to grant him a wife, so children may be born in the land to the east. Totson, however, is jealous of Yako's song, his many attributes and his magical powers. He refuses to welcome Yako to his village. Instead he disappears into his underground dwelling to ready his throwing stick, arrows and magic war spear so that he can kill the friendly Yako.

The women of the village, having heard Yako's song, are pleased but frightened. The wife of the second chief of the village offers Yako her daughter, the child Tsukala, and warns him of his danger. The women of the village then become jealous and try to prevent Tsukala's mother from giving her daughter to the handsome and mighty youth. Yako extends his magic paddle to the beach and has her mother place Tsukala upon it. He draws it back and places Tsukala upon a bed of sheep's wool inside the canoe. As the village women raise their clubs to strike Tsukala's mother, Yako creates a magic wave that casts her to safety and overwhelms the threatening women.

Totson, rushing out, casts spears and arrows after the fleeing Yako. Then he raises a storm, hoping to destroy Yako's light canoe with wind and waves. This failing, he pursues Yako in his skin war boat with his war bow, arrows, spears and throwing stick, riding the wild sea waves. Using his powerful magic, Totson increases the size and strength of the waves in a greater attempt to destroy Yako's canoe. Yako, however, is a more powerful magician and he carries a wave-quelling stone, which he sends skipping ahead. Where the stone passes the waters are stilled, opening a path of quiet water for Yako's canoe to pass through, while Totson must labor through stormy seas in pursuit. Even so, the Raven chief follows rapidly and gains upon Yako. Guided by Yako's streaming black hair, Totson shoots all of his arrows and throws all of his spears to no avail.

Finally he attempts to kill Yako with his great war spear, which never fails. He throws his spear directly at Yako's exposed back. Yako, seeing the shining spear flying through the air, calls upon his most powerful magic. He changes a great wave that is approaching Totson into a mountain of stone. The war spear strikes its crest and glances upward with the crash of breaking rock. The mighty spear flies higher, impelled by the strength of Totson's throw, sailing over the quiet waters until it reaches the crest of a still greater wave. Yako immediately turns this wave into a greater mountain of stone. The spear is again deflected and flies high into the southern sky to land among the stars.

Totson, the mighty warrior of blood-stained hands, then meets disaster. His war boat crashes into the mountain of stone and he is thrown onto the rocks. There he is instantly changed into a raven. Dripping from the sea waters and without weapons, the transformed Totson flies to the top of the new, magically formed, mountain. Exhausted from his exertions, Yako falls into a deep sleep. When he wakes, he finds himself at his home camp in a spruce forest. Tsukala has grown into a woman and she has prepared food for him. Yako gazes around him and sees the great mountains he created from the waves of the sea. The greater one, which had sent Totson's spear into the stars, came to be called Denali, the High One. The lesser mountain, first struck by Totson's war spear, is traditionally known by the Native people as "Totson-to-kadatlkoitan." The path of water quieted by the skipping stone became the valleys of the Yukon and Tanana Rivers, the home of the descendants of Yako and Tsukala. Their children, taught by their parents to live in peace, justice and plenty, would, in their generations, migrate far to the east and south.

Another chief, from the Porcupine region, tells of a period following this time of early creation. He speaks of the time when Naradkaka (the creator-god), great-horned bison and mammoths wandered the land and a great lake named Mun-na filled part of the Yukon Valley. It was a time of plenty when Kaath, the king salmon and his cousin, Whokadza, spawned in the shallows of the lake, while Dinnaji, the bull moose, fed on the tubers of water lilies along its shores and summer nests surrounding the lake held Toba, the swan; Tunsa, the snipe; Dilkuu, the robin; and Delthowa, the warbler. Then came the day when Dzadukaka, the dread northern spirit of cold, looked upon this happy land. His heart was filled with envy and he caused his flame-bearer, Yoyekoi, the Aurora Borealis, to report the source of the people's happiness. Upon learning that it came from the warmth of Mun-na and the great forests, he caused the north wind to blow fiercely, snow to form deep glaciers and ice to form in Mun-na. The giant animals all froze to death, leaving their bones where they are found today when annual floods wash away river banks.

In the south, Roletkaka, the spirit of heat, whose flame-bearer is Sa, the sun, saw this and determined he would restore the frozen land. These powerful shamans caused warm winds to blow and sent warm floods to melt the snow and ice, for Sa has greater power than Yoyekoi of the northern lights. Mun-na, the great lake, was, however, destroyed forever. In assisting Roletkaka, mighty rivers filled the deeps of the lake with silt and sand. Forests grew upon the alluvial plane and plenty was restored to the people of the land. The crest of Denali is considered to be the throne of Sa, the solar shaman and Master of Life. Annually he conquers Dzadu of the north, the demon of snow, and renews life with warming rains, green growth, spawning fish, migrating waterfowl, roaming caribou, sheep, moose and animals awakened from their winter's sleep.

Though not commonly known, this great mountain is considered to be a major global power point. In the tradition of the Great White Brotherhood, it acts as a reception, anchoring and transmittal center of cosmic energies related to spiritual evolution on Earth.

Directions

Denali National Park is located 120 miles (194 km) south of Fairbanks and 240 miles (387 km) north of Anchorage. It is accessible by air, rail, bus or highway. To arrange air transportation contact ERA Aviation/Alaska Airlines at (800) 426-0333 or Continental USA and Hawaii at (907) 243-3300 in Anchorage.

For a scenic trip by rail, contact the Alaska Railroad Corporation, Passenger Service, P.O. Box 107500, Anchorage, AK 99510-7500, or call (907) 265-2494 (Anchorage), (907) 456-4155 (Fairbanks) or (800) 544-0552 (Continental USA and Hawaii).

Bus service to the park is provided by several companies. Travel arrangements can be made with Denali Express at (800) 327-7651 or (907) 274-8539, Anchorage; Alaska Sightseeing Tours at (907) 276-1305, Anchorage, or (907) 452-8518, Fairbanks; or Grey Line of Alaska/Westours at (907) 277-5581, Anchorage or (907) 456-7741, Fairbanks.

You can also drive to the park. Private vehicles are not usually permitted past the Savage River Campground, fifteen miles (25 km) inside of the park. Shuttle buses are provided on a daily schedule, leaving frequently from the Visitor Access Center near park headquarters and traveling to Eielson Visitor Center and Wonder Lake. The buses make scheduled stops, as well as occasional breaks to view wildlife. You may get off the bus en route, except in closed areas, and may change buses as desired. During the peak season of July and August buses may be crowded. After the close of the season, usually following Labor Day, bus service may not be offered. A private vehicle may be needed to access the interior of the park at this time (they are allowed when public transportation is not available). Gasoline is not available on inner park roads.

The one-way bus trip to Wonder Lake takes about five-and-a-half hours and food service is not available, so take along food and drink. Weather during the summer can be wet, windy and cool, with temperatures ranging from 35°F to 75°F (2°C to 24°C). Warm clothing and rain gear are necessary. Good footwear and insect repellent are advisable, though by September the rainy season is normally over and usually insects are greatly reduced. Unpredictable weather in May, early June and mid-September may delay or hasten the opening and closing dates of park roads and facilities. Recorded information regarding conditions is available by calling (907) 683-2686.

For the hearty, back-country permits are sometimes available from park headquarters during the winter. Dog-sled passenger trips are offered by Denali Dog Tours, P.O. Box 670, Denali National Park, AK 99755.

Information

Information and literature are available from the Visitor Access Center located near the entrance to the park. The admission fee is $3 per person, with those under 17 or over 62 and the disabled admitted free of charge.

Free back-country permits for overnight camping must be obtained from this center. Information regarding areas of the park that are closed for hiking, due to activities by bears or other wildlife, is provided by the Visitor Access Center.

Information by mail is also available from the Superintendent, Denali National Park and Preserve, PO Box 9, Denali Park, AK 99755. A free list of maps and other publications is available from the Alaska Natural History Association, PO Box 838, Denali Park, AK 99755.

General information plus interesting displays and films are provided by Alaska Public Lands Information Centers. These are at 250 Cushman St., Fairbanks, AK 99707, (907) 451-7352 or, for deaf access, (907) 451-7439; and at 605 West 4th Ave., Anchorage, AK 99501, (907) 271-2737, or for deaf access, (907) 271-2738.

Source Notes

Denali, National Park Service, U.S. Department of the Interior, GPO: 1990-262-100/20031 Reprint 1990.

Wickersham, Hon. James. *Old Yukon*, Washington D.C.: Washington Law Book Co., 1938, p. 243.

Bailey, Alice. *The Externalization of the Hierarchy*, Lucis Publishing Co., 1972, p. 142

Bailey, Alice. *Discipleship in the New Age*, Lucis Publishing Co., 1972, p. 123.

The Lost City of the Arctic
Frank Joseph

There is no more desolate nor uninhabitable place on our planet than above the Arctic Circle. Ferocious temperatures lashed by blasting windstorms make it the most difficult area for life to get a foothold. This ultimately remote and forbidding polar region would be the last place anyone would expect to discover evidence for an ancient civilization. Yet, the distinguished *Natural History* magazine reported, "We have now found an Arctic metropolis many times larger than anything previously thought possible in this part of the world and inhabited by people whose material culture differed markedly from that of the Eskimos, as we know them."

With these words, F. G. Rainey announced the discovery of a mystery still to be explained. In June, 1940, he and fellow archaeologist, Magnus Marks, returned for further excavations at Ipiutak, on Point Hope, in northern Alaska. In the Yupik dialect spoken by Natives of western Alaska, *ipiutak* means seal tusk. Two years before, they found tell-tale signs there of an ancient settlement in faint lines on the permafrost, and assumed it was no different from other, primitive, small communities of fishing peoples, the direct ancestors of the Eskimos, perhaps 500 years ago. The scientists' third season, however, would reveal something entirely different and unprecedented. They noticed that this year the grass and moss were greener and more distinct than before, perhaps due to subterranean organic refuse which caused growth above any buried structures to appear more distinct against the surrounding plain.

Following along the outlines of the buried features, they could clearly distinguish long boulevards of square foundations spreading east and west across the north shore. "We became aware of the astonishing extent of the ruins," Rainey said. He and Magnus excitedly traced the figures of large, square buildings regularly arranged along five main avenues and down short cross-blocks, where smaller structures, suggestive of houses, stood at right angles to the thoroughfares. Their finished survey identified more than 600 buildings, but incomplete test pits indicated at least another 200. The buried town is less than a quarter-mile across and nearly a mile long, with an original population of some 4,000 residents, larger by far than anything known to the Eskimos, who, in any case, never built such structures or evidenced the city planning apparent at the site. Moreover, in the twenty-three buildings excavated by Rainey and Marks, nothing they found resembled anything familiar to the local natives. "One of the most striking features of the Ipiutak material is the elaborate and sophisticated carving and the beautiful workmanship, which would not be expected in a primitive, proto-Eskimo culture ancestral to the modern."

Another researcher, Rene Noorbergen, writes that the prehistoric inhabitants of Ipiutak "had a knowledge of mathematics and astronomy comparable to that of the ancient Mayas." The absence of any large refuge deposits covering the buildings, which were not superimposed over older structures, showed that the town was simultaneously occupied by its inhabitants and did not slowly develop over time. Every indication of the physical evidence demonstrated that Ipiutak was raised all at once and occupied by the same people who built it. Who they were remains a puzzling enigma. Excavators of their cemetery found the remains of tall, slender individuals with traces of blond hair and skulls similar to Cro-Magnon remains common in Western Europe. Clearly, they were not related to the Eskimos.

Their preferred artistic design was the spiral composed of two elements carved in the round. The motif appears nowhere else in America, but is found on the other side of the Pacific Ocean among the ancient Caucasoid Ainu of Japan and the Amur River tribes in northeastern Asia. The great distances separating this symbol common to such diverse peoples suggests to some investigators that all were directly descended from the great civilization of Mu, lost beneath the Pacific in a terrible catastrophe several millennia ago. Indeed, the underground site at Ipiutak is sunk in deep antiquity. Rainey and Marks found it "buried beneath so much sand from the beach" that the city must have flourished thousands of years in the past.

Even more than the anomalous appearance of a sophisticated society flourishing in an area otherwise entirely known for its small bands of Eskimo hunters trying to scratch out an existence, the profound age of the discovery is especially upsetting to our understanding of prehistory. Ipiutak could only have been inhabited when warmer conditions allowed for a civilization to survive and prosper there. But such conditions did not exit at Point Hope for the last 30,000 years, a time when man, we are told, produced nothing like a city. Archaeologists conclude that northern Alaska must have been ice-free with a temperate climate, missed by the glaciers which were carving up the rest of North America. Theirs is speculation only, and actually contrary to what geologists know about the last ice age.

"However," explorer David Hatcher Childress writes, "it is difficult to see how a large ice cap from an ice age would leave a huge swathe of semitropical land extending into the unaccountably ice-free Arctic seas adjacent to the pole. Add to this the large population now said to be encamped on these shores over 10,000 years ago, and we have a historical puzzle that would make any geologist, archaeologist or historian clench his teeth." It seems clear that the mile-long habitation site at Ipiutak was built before the last glaciation, thus suggesting a civilized antiquity far beyond our expectation or accepted chronologies.

Mystical Significance

The popular historian, Will Durant, wrote, "Immense volumes have been written to expound our knowledge, and conceal our ignorance, of primitive man. Primitive cultures were not necessarily the ancestors of our own; for all we know, they may be the degenerate remnants of higher cultures that decayed when human leadership moved in the wake of the ice." Durant's words recall the old Norse myth of the origins of humankind, when Abdumla, the sacred cow, licked away the ice of a glacier to form the first man and woman. The Greeks, too, had a myth of Hyperboria, a place north of Oceanus, near the North Pole, strangely known for its perpetual springtime, despite the constant cold. The Hyperborean maidens were a select group of priestesses, who traveled from their polar homeland to the sacred island of Delos, where they came to worship at the birthplace of Apollo. Their tombs are still pointed out among the classical ruins by tour guides on the Aegean island.

This is not to suggest the permafrost remains at Ipiutak represent ancient Hyperboria. They do, however, indicate that a civilization unlike anything produced by the Eskimo culture did indeed thrive in the Arctic at least 10,000 years ago. And it may have been a ceremonial center, in view of some of the ritual objects excavated. Among the outstanding examples, as mentioned above, are repeated instances of the sacred spiral, generally interpreted to signify the journey of the soul through time, from birth to death and rebirth, just as the infant leaves its mother's womb in a spiral motion. Another material symbol found at Ipiutak was a human skull with ivory nose plugs and an ivory cover over the mouth. The sockets were inserted with ivory carvings resembling eyes inlaid with polished stone pupils, giving the skull a lifelike appearance. The modified skull underscores its companion spiral carvings as a symbol of rebirth. Installing open eyes, signifying life, into a death's head (its breath stopped at nostrils and mouth), implies concepts of an afterlife not native to the Arctic.

We may infer from these and similar artifacts that the ancient residents of Ipiutak were practitioners of a mystery cult, whose rituals emphasized the eternal conquest of the soul over recurring episodes of death. As more excavations succeed in making new discoveries at the Arctic city, a ceremonial center as spiritually resonant as it is profoundly ancient may arise to challenge the heads and hearts of modern humans. That such a place did indeed exist an incredible 130 miles (210 km) north of the Arctic Circle makes the Ipiutak site one of the most enigmatic on Earth.

Directions

Individual excursions to Point Hope are not recommended, save for well-equipped, professional explorers. However, organized trips are available from the following services: Alaska Airlines, tel. 1-800-426-0333; Arctic Air Guides, tel. (907) 442-3030; Tour Arctic, tel. (907)

442-3301; Alaska Sightseeing Tours, tel. 1-800-666-7365; Mark Tours, tel. 1-800-478-0800.

Information

Superintendent, Northwest Alaska Areas, National Park Service, PO Box 1029, Kotzebue, AK 99752; tel. (907) 442-3760.

Source Notes

Rainey, Froelich G. "Mystery People of the Arctic," *Natural History*, New York: Natural History, Inc., 1941, 46: pp. 148–155+.

Childress, David Hatcher. *Lost Cities of North & Central America*, Stelle, Illinois: Adventures Unlimited Press, 1992, pp. 569–571.

Noorbergen, Rene. *Secrets of Lost Races*, New York: Barnes & Noble Publishers, 1977.

Alberta

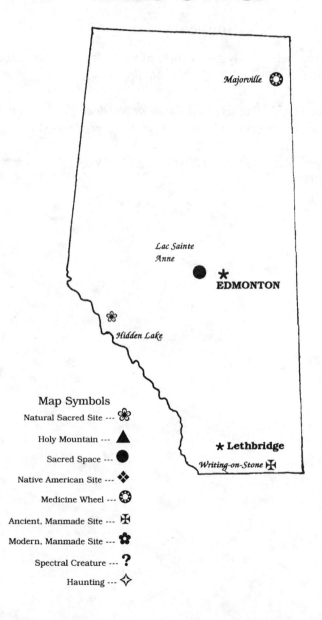

Majorville ✵

Lac Sainte
Anne
● ★
EDMONTON

❀
Hidden Lake

★ **Lethbridge**

Writing-on-Stone ✠

Map Symbols

Natural Sacred Site --- ❀

Holy Mountain --- ▲

Sacred Space --- ●

Native American Site --- ❖

Medicine Wheel --- ✵

Ancient, Manmade Site --- ✠

Modern, Manmade Site --- ✿

Spectral Creature --- **?**

Haunting --- ◇

Writing-on-Stone
Frank Joseph

When settlers began pushing through south Alberta in the early nineteenth century, they unexpectedly entered a barren, lunarlike landscape of gargantuan natural formations. Weirdly fashioned by eons of erosion, the colossi resembled nothing human, but suggested the monuments of an extinct race of titans. Some resembled monstrous toadstools. The first visitors called these formations "hoodoos" for the ghostly sensations they generated in observers.

Ranging in height from only a few inches to more than fifty feet, the hoodoos initially were roughly sculpted by ancient torrents of the nearby Milk River, then were finished by a million years of wind action. Their sombrerolike caps are harder conglomerate that resist the elements which erode the softer stone on which they perch. The pillars wear their old story in colored bands of brown and gray; the former marks the levels of vanished seas impregnated with countless fossils, while the latter were left by the vast swamps that covered Alberta when dinosaurs ruled Canada. Sometimes these skeletal remnants are visible within the stone matrix of the hoodoos themselves, lending the mushroomlike towers an even more bizarre aspect.

Early visitors were awed by the magical silence that lay like a spell over the badlands, so named by the first French-Canadian trappers who arrived in the late seventeenth century. They referred to the area as *mauvaises terres pour traverser*, or "bad lands for crossing." In the years following, the term was applied to other similarly eroded topography sharing some of the fantastically shaped features fashioned by time and elements. This impressive milieu was underscored by the desiccated remains of human corpses occasionally encountered along the way. For generations, the Sheshone Indians used the area as a cemetery, a holy place where the dead resided before moving on to the higher regions of the Great Spirit. As such, both Natives and newcomers regarded the badlands as haunted, and both rarely entered the hallowed precinct carved out by the Earth Mother as a place of death and transfiguration.

As the settlers cautiously made their way in the shadows of towering hoodoos, they found themselves facing the Milk River, so named by the

31

famous explorers Lewis and Clark because its waters reminded them of tea with milk. Rising in Montana, it is the only river in Canada to flow southward, emptying into the distant Gulf of Mexico. And it was this once-great stream that, many millions of years ago, carved out the deep-walled canyonland. But on either side of the lovely, gently meandering river visitors were amazed to find its steep cliffs adorned with a huge natural canvas of illustrations etched deeply into the sandstone. The images covered hundreds of feet across the cliff-face. Doubtless, they were older than anyone could guess; their creation seemed to represent an accumulation of effort spanning time. That they were part of the sacred landscape was obvious at first sight.

There were depictions of warriors, hunters, recognizable animals, fantastic beings, geometric designs and glyphlike characters of which the Indian residents knew little. True, the Sheshones' mark was on the Milk River sandstone, but their contribution to the vast art work was relatively small. Unknown others, unguessed generations before them, were responsible for most of the enigmatic illustrations. Who these earliest artists may have been, from whence they came and what became of them have perplexed investigators of the site ever since.

B.C. Writing-on-Stone.   *Photo by Frank Joseph.*

Today Writing-on-Stone is a 1,055-acre (422-hectare) provincial park, sixty miles southeast of Lethbridge, five miles above the U.S. border at Montana. With fifty-eight separate, related sites, it comprises the largest display of rock paintings and carvings in North America, and perhaps in the world. Its images range from the starkly primitive to the symmetrically sophisticated. The perfection of the circles (representing warrior shields) could only have been achieved by means of a compass, probably a pin-and-thong affair. More intriguing, large shields were never used by the Sheshone, nor any known tribal people in Alberta. To some investigators, the portrayed shield-bearing warriors are more akin to soldiers of the ancient European Bronze Age (circa 1200 B.C.) than anything Native. Indeed, as early as 1855, the first person to document Writing-on-Stone, James Doty, was told by Sheshone elders that the oldest inscriptions were made by white men who arrived many years before the modern immigrants.

Tradition to the contrary, other researchers, such as Henriette Mertz, see in the rock carvings evidence of Chinese visitors arriving in Canada 4,200 years ago on behalf of Emperor Shu. Interestingly, at least a few of the designs do in fact resemble Chinese characters of the early first millennium B.C., while much of the West Coast territory seems reflected in the chronicle of a Buddhist monk, Hwui Shan, who described a trans-pacific land to the distant east he called Fu-Sang. At the very least, these theories demonstrate the fascination Writing-on-Stone continues to exert on the human imagination.

Mystical Significance

The tremendous variety of the art work at Writing-on-Stone suggests that there is no single meaning or interpretation that can explain the whole site. This is especially true when we consider that successive generations of artists belonging to different tribes (or even races, if we are to believe Doty, Mertz, et al.) made their own, singular contributions, which may have had little or nothing to do with those who came before and after. Some of the images, such as those portraying warriors, appear to depict military exploits and conquests. Others seem like attempts to document visions, illustrating the highlights of expanded consciousness. Many seem to represent efforts at conjuring spirit guardians. Judging from the awe-inspiring atmosphere of the place, they succeeded.

For the modern visitor, Writing-on-Stone is a place of communion between nature and mankind, where an extraordinary environment was long ago recognized by those subtle, intuitive facilities of an ancient shaman. It was here, at this unique spot of extinct beasts, lost seas and human ghosts, that the otherworld of the spirit created a bridge into our material plain. The bridge still exists for our use. Its fabulous, mysterious rock carvings are prehistoric mandalas that open upon the soul's journey to a higher consciousness.

Directions

From Lethbridge, take Highway 4 south to the town of Milk River. Then take 501 east twenty miles (32 km) (watch for signs) to Writing-on-Stone.

Source Notes

Magne, P. R. Martin & Klassen, Michael A. "A Multivariate Study of Rock Art Anthropomorphs at Writing-on-Stone, Southern Alberta," *American Antiquity,* 1991, 56 (3): pp. 389–418.

Keener, J. D. "Writing-on-Stone: Rock Art on the Northwestern Plains," *Canadian Journal of Archaeology,* 1977, 1:15–80.

Mertz, Henrietta. *Gods from the Far East: How the Chinese Discovered America,* NY: Ballasting Books, 1972.

Lac Sainte Anne
Frank Joseph

Some thirty-two miles (50 km) east of Edmonton lies a small body of water, pleasant but apparently not unlike any of Alberta's other lakes. Eleven months out of the year, it attracts a few visitors who enjoy solitude and outdoor relaxation, just as they might at one of the many public parks in the vicinity. But for five days every July, the shores of Lac Sainte Anne are transformed by crowds of more than 10,000 people.

They come from around the province and throughout North America. Others arrive from the far corners of the world. Many of the persons who often travel great distances are afflicted in soul, mind or body. They are drawn in a solemn pilgrimage to this otherwise unoutstanding place for an annual renewal generated by the sacred character of the lake itself. Their convocation also commemorates an event that took place more than 100 years ago.

Before the turn of the last century, Alberta was afflicted by the worst drought in its history. The land and its inhabitants suffered through months of unrelieved misery. By midsummer, adverse conditions were becoming intolerable. In July, a Roman Catholic missionary was surprised to notice unusually large numbers of birds and other animals massing at Lac Sainte Anne. Many of these creatures appeared to be suffering from various ailments. But after drinking or splashing at the shore, they seemed revived and strengthened. Why did they gather here, and not at the other lakes, he wondered? He shared his observations with fellow priests at the local mission, where they had been praying for an end to the drought for many weeks. They decided to renew their prayers at the edge of Lac Sainte Anne, where so many animals sought relief from trouble. Their mysterious presence seemed like a kind of guidance. After five days and nights of uninterrupted supplications, the drought suddenly came to an end.

Ever since, growing numbers of celebrants, of all religious persuasions, congregate at Lac Sainte Anne as a place where prayers are answered. It is at this time, during the annual five-day commemoration, that the waters are said to take on special curative properties less in evidence throughout the rest of the year. The lake has a reputation for healing that continues to attract sufferers from near and far.

Mystical Significance

The Lourdes of Alberta as Lac Sainte Anne is sometimes known, was sacred long before the Roman Catholic missionaries used its shores from which to pray for assistance against drought. It was revered by generations of Native Canadians preceding the Christian arrival as Spirit Lake or Big Medicine Lake, for the healing power of its waters. Tribal peoples believed it had been especially set aside by the Earth Mother to nurture all her children, animals as well as humans. So the appearance of so many birds at Big Medicine Lake during a time of trouble did not surprise resident Indians. It is interesting to learn, however, that two different peoples espousing separate, even contradictory religious views, were led to venerate the same hallowed location. Their human response to a place of telluric power confirms its validity as an active sacred site.

Although its waters display year-round curative properties, only during the five-day commemoration each mid-July do they evidence the kind of healing potential regarded as miraculous by more than a century of pilgrims. Although scientific explanations about large mineral contents undoubtedly explain the basis for the lake's medicinal effects, the accumulated spiritual power generated by 10,000 persons focused on the resident *genius loci* creates a very real effect on the higher level of cures at Lac Saint Anne. It is this human interplay with the concentrated power of the Earth that creates a genuine and potent sacred center.

Directions

From Edmonton, take Highway 16 going east. At Spruce Grove, go north on Highway 43 about six miles (10 km) to a sign indicating Lac Sainte Anne on the left (east).

Information

Edmonton Tourism, 9797 Jasper Ave., Edmonton, AB T5J 1N9; tel. (403) 496-8400, or (800) 463-4667.

Source Notes

Lightbody, Mark and Tom Smalltown. *Canada, a Travel Survival Kit*, London: Lonely Planet Publications, 1992, p. 534.

Hidden Lake
Frank Joseph

The largest glacier-fed lake in the Rockies and the second largest in the world lies about thirty miles (48 km) southeast of Jasper. Ringed by cathedral-like peaks, Maligne Lake is about fifteen miles (22km) in length and encompasses some of the most perfectly blue water on Earth. Native Canadians knew it as Chaba Imne, the Hidden Lake, and so it remained as late as 1908, when it was discovered by a female explorer, Mary Schaffer.

Today, the location is far from concealed. It attracts bus-loads of hikers, anglers, trail riders and white-water rafters from all over Alberta and beyond. So much so, crowds of people with nothing on their minds but having a good time can be distracting, especially in high season. Whatever magic the place once possessed has been driven out by the onslaught of big business tourism.

Downstream from the profaned body of water, however, the Maligne

River flows into Medicine Lake. Investigators believe it may be the original Chaba Imne due to the nature of its strange behavior. In spring, Medicine Lake is five miles (8 km) long and fifty-five feet (20 m) deep. But in autumn it utterly vanishes, leaving only a dry gravel bed to mark its former location throughout the winter. This may be the real meaning of a hidden lake.

The site is reached via a clearly designated hiking trail that leads from Maligne Lake. It follows along the Maligne River through charming alpine meadows and dramatic waterfalls to offer thrilling panoramas of the surrounding mountain ranges. The trail goes on to skirt Maligne Canyon, a 150-foot-deep (50 m) gorge sculpted through limestone bedrock by the thundering river during unknown millennia. Passing across six-foot (2 m) bridges, visitors may reach Medicine Lake in a two-hour round-trip over the two-mile (4 km) interpretive pathway.

Mystical Significance

The annual disappearance and reappearance of Medicine Lake is a unique natural wonder. Scientists speculate that a system of subterranean drainage caves are responsible for its behavior, but they are still unable to account for the general regularity of its seasonal coming and going. Resident Natives were more confident that all natural phenomena were the physical manifestations of underlying spiritual forces. In other words, God's will was visible in the laws of Nature.

Various tribal peoples who resided throughout the Maligne area into historic times regarded the canyon and its two lakes with special awe. No villages or burials were ever set up in their vicinity. The location was not tabu, however. Shamans, the spiritual leaders of the community, often made pilgrimages along the same trail used today by tourists to partake of the manitou, or mystical energy of Nature, so much in evidence throughout the area. Thus empowered, the shamans returned among their people to cure them of physical and mental ills and provided them with visions of the future. Medicine Lake derives its name from these solitary pilgrimages.

But the healing implied in the name was not limited to aboriginal medical practices. The cures sought at Hidden Lake administered first to the soul, because treating the body without first making the spirit whole would, at best, result only in a temporary alleviation of distress. Spiritual pain manifested itself in physical illness; one could not be healthy if the other was unwell. It is in this mystical interdependence of the Seen and the Unseen that the true significance of things hidden may be applied to Medicine Lake.

Its paralleling the tides of seasonal change alone inspires mystical reactions. Each springtide ushers into the world the revival of life, accompanied by the reappearance of the waters. And as Earth takes on the trappings of wintery death, so too, the lake vanishes, leaving a barren stretch of lifeless gravel. But, miraculously, it revives with the vernal equinox. The holiness of this cycle is at Medicine Lake exemplified in a way found nowhere else, and therefore, all the more powerfully.

Directions

From Edmonton, take Highway 16 west into Jasper National Park. Arriving in the town of Jasper, take the Jasper Park access road. Signs here clearly mark the way to Maligne Lake.

Source Notes

Bouillon, J. *North American Natural Heritage*, New York: Baker Publishers, Inc., 1925.

Randolf, Reginald. *Canadian Phenomena*, Toronto: Yorkshire Press Ltd., 1946.

British Columbia

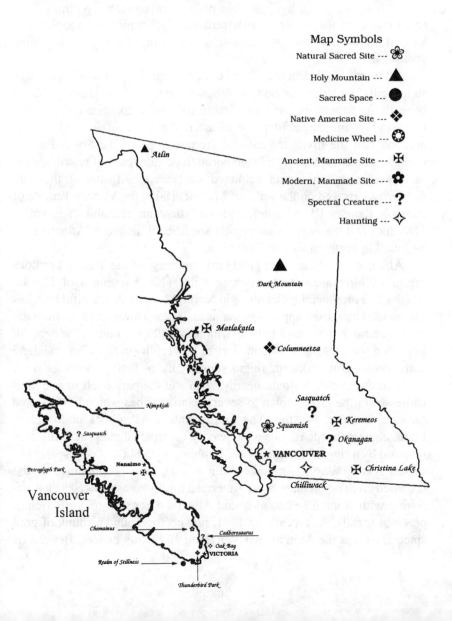

Map Symbols

Natural Sacred Site --- ✿

Holy Mountain --- ▲

Sacred Space --- ●

Native American Site --- ◆

Medicine Wheel --- ✸

Ancient, Manmade Site --- ✠

Modern, Manmade Site --- ✿

Spectral Creature --- ?

Haunting --- ✦

▲ Atlin

▲ Dark Mountain

✠ Matlakatla

◆ Columneetza

Sasquatch ?

✠ Keremeos

✿ Squamish

? Okanagan

★ VANCOUVER

◆ Nimpkish

? Sasquatch

✦ Chilliwack

✠ Christina Lake

Petroglyph Park

Nanaimo ★ ✠

Vancouver
Island

Chemainus

Cadborosaurus

✦ Oak Bay

◆★ VICTORIA

Realm of Stillness

●

Thunderbird Park

Atlantis in Canada
Frank Joseph

The great motherland of civilization was allegedly destroyed more than 3,000 years ago by a terrible natural catastrophe. Nothing of it remains, save the ancient oral traditions of numerous peoples unknown to each other and separated by many thousands of miles around the world.

Although located in the Atlantic Ocean, the Empire of Atlantis was supposedly a worldwide power. When a cataclysm of nature pulled it beneath the waves, its survivors fled to its former colonies and beyond. Even today, millennia after the disaster, the story of lost Atlantis is preserved in the myths of cultures from Europe to the South Pacific. Canada is no exception. The Petersborough petroglyphs of Ontario appear to represent the ships and helmeted warriors of Atlantis as they are similarly portrayed on the walls of Medinet Habu, the Victory Temple of Pharaoh Ramses III, who defeated the Atlantean invasion of Egypt in 1187 B.C. But the only Canadian site specifically linked to Atlantis may be found in northern British Columbia.

About ninety-four miles (150 km) southeast of the Yukon Territory capital, Whitehorse, and sixty-three miles (100 km) north of Juneau, Alaska, is a provincial park unique in North America. A beautiful lake lies surrounded by snow-capped mountains and a deep forest. Not far from the lake, natural hot springs bubble with 85°F (29°C) mineral water. An imposing summit, Birch Mountain, rises powerfully to form Teresa Island at the center of the lake and reigns supreme as the highest point for fresh water in the world. A small, nearby town and the park itself derive their names from the lake, known to several Native tribes which have passed through the area, as Atlin. The fourth-century B.C. Greek philosopher, Plato, characterized Atlantis as a heavily forested island practically surrounded by a ring of mountains and bubbling with hot and cold springs of sacred water. Was it for Lake Atlin's suggestive resemblance to the drowned civilization that Native American traditions associated its natural setting with Atlantis? Plato also said Atlantis was extraordinarily rich in precious metals. As recently as 1981, prospectors found a chunk of gold since known as the Atlin nugget, weighing 36.86 troy ounces. Beyond its physical similarity to Plato's description and the obvious Atlantean parallel of its name, Atlin was and is regarded as a sacred site by various regional tribes, some of whom still commemorate the oral tradition of the Great Flood, appropriately enough.

In a variant remarkably similar to the same account repeated by every North American tribe, the Salish perpetuate a folk memory in song of a splendid lodge in the Sunrise Sea, very long ago. Although wealthy, its residents were sinful, so the gods set the lodge on fire with a star thrown from the sky. In dire distress, the people implored heaven to put out the fire. "When the gods wish to punish us," their wise man cried, "they answer our prayers," for just then the lodge sank into the sea with most of its inhabitants. Those who survived, climbed onto the back of a giant turtle, who brought them safely to a new place. They called it Turtle Island, the Indian name for North America, in honor of their early benefactor. From these survivors all Native Americans claim descent.

Several petroglyphs meant to portray the turtle, the animal-hero of the Great Flood, may still be found not far from the shores of Atlin.

Mystical Significance

Atlin's philological roots, its general physical resemblance to Plato's sunken city and Native American tales of the Great Flood still commemorated at the park define the lake as an Atlantean sacred site. But the world-wide magnitude of that catastrophe touched all mankind, not just a few Indian tribes. It is in their oral histories, however, that the story of Atlantis is still preserved. Among the essential ingredients of any sacred site is its power to excite a sense of wonder in those who come to feel themselves nurtured by it.

Atlin excels in this fundamental prerequisite because of its Atlantean setting, a natural simulacrum chosen by the bearers of the Atlantis tradition for its physical resemblance to the lost homeland of civilized humanity. When we approach such a place with an open mind and heart, the parallel environment speaks to us at profoundly inner levels of knowing often beyond verbal expression. Our genetic and/or karmic memories of former lives we lived in that most splendid kingdom long swallowed beneath the sea may be rekindled into remembrance of times past. Certainly, sympathetic visitors to Lake Atlin often feel on the verge of memory. As such, the site is an ideal one for past-life regressions of all kinds, aided and abetted, as such deeply introspective procedures are, by the stimulating surroundings and the ceremonial energies drummed into the parallel landscape for numerous generations.

Atlantean past-life recall is particularly valuable to members of the present generation, not only because we thereby obtain a heightened sense of identity. It is even more important for us to grasp the awful historical comparisons between the self-destructive fate of ancient Atlantis and the present world-wide crisis posed by our civilization.

Directions

Atlin Provincial Park is located in the northwest corner of British Columbia. From Whitehorse, take Highway 2 at Jake's Corner south following posted signs directly to Atlin. To reach Whitehorse by air (two hours by car from Atlin), see Canadian Airlines (604-668-3535) for daily flights from Calgary and Vancouver. Daily round-trip bus (Greyhound, 604-667-2223) from Edmonton is $380. There is a regular bus run from Whitehorse to Atlin Mondays, Wednesdays and Fridays via the Atlin Express. For reservations, telephone Atlin Express in advance (250-651-7617).

Information

Atlin Historical Museum (showcases Tingit Indian artifacts), corner of 3rd & Trainor Streets. Telephone (250) 651-7522. Open mid-May to mid-September, daily, 10 A.M. to 6 P.M. With special thanks to Judith Voswinkel, President, Atlin Visitors Association, Box 365, Atlin, B.C. V0W 1A0. Telephone (250) 651-7603; fax (250) 651-7757.

Source Notes

Donnelly, Ignatius. *Atlantis, The Antediluvian World*, New York, New York: Gramercy Publishing Company, 1985.

Joseph, Frank. *Atlantis in Wisconsin*, Lakeville, Minnesota: Galde Press, Inc., 1995.

The Cadborosaurus of Victoria

Frank Joseph

Among the best documented so-called sea monsters is a beast seen by more than a thousand eyewitnesses in Victoria's Cadboro Bay since 1933. Although unofficial reports went back to the nineteenth century and even earlier sightings were made by local Natives, the creature's first verified encounter took place on October 8, 1933. Major W. H. Langley was sailing his sloop, *Dorothy*, not far from Chatham Island on that Sunday afternoon, at about 1:30.

He was a highly respected barrister and serving at the time as clerk of the B.C. Legislature. The Major was, moreover, a seasoned navigator, having spent a nine-month tour aboard a whaling ship. Langley described the monster this way: "It was every bit as big as a whale, but entirely different from a whale in many respects. I believe the serpent was nearly eighty feet long and as wide as the average automobile. It was greenish brown in color, with a serrated body. My vessel was about a hundred feet away from the creature when it appeared. Water conditions at the time were relatively calm, with a light wind from the south west." He said the monster's head resembled that of a camel.

The following month, it was seen again by a local fisherman. "It was like a big water snake," John F. Murray was quoted as saying. "He swam exactly like a worm would and I watched him go for about sixty feet with about two feet of his head and neck out of the water." The entire sighting lasted perhaps three minutes, a very long time for Murray to get a clear view of the sea-beast. He saw it from a distance of perhaps seventy-five feet (25m), an encounter even closer than Major Langley's experience. The November sighting was made at Ogden Point, near its breakwater. Although Murray was a less illustrious eyewitness than the Major, his story made international news.

Two separate and very clear sightings of the creature later named Cadborosaurus were made early the following year, not at Cadboro Bay, but further north at Gulf Island and South Pender Island. On the morning of February 4th, 1934, Cyril H. Andrews and Norman Georgeson were hunting along the shore toward Gowland Head. Around 11:00 A.M., they saw a huge serpentlike creature gliding slowly just below the water. A duck they shot in midflight fell to the surface, where the monster suddenly raised part of its body, followed by its head, opened its jaws and swallowed the duck whole. Andrews stood only ten feet from the beast. While devouring its meal, many sea gulls descended on the Cadborosaurus, which made vain attempts to catch one of the birds in its mouth, then sank abruptly under the water. About thirty minutes later, the creature reappeared only fifty-six feet from shore. As before, its head and part of the undulating body were visible, this time by a local justice of the peace and a dozen other South Pender Island residents. Both Andrews and Georgeson swore out a joint affidavit affirming their sighting.

By 1950, more than 500 eyewitnesses had filed reports with the Victoria authorities. Forty years later, reports have tripled. The descriptions are remarkably consistent in depicting the monster as serpentlike and mottled dark green in color. Only estimates of its overall length vary drastically from thirty-five to one hundred and ten feet. Before the outbreak of World War II, qualified, even professional observers (city officials, military personnel, newspaper reporters, etc.) provided so many quality eyewitness accounts, that the reality of the creature was accepted by local scientific authorities.

Unlike their overseas' colleagues confronted by the similar Loch Ness phenomenon, the Canadian scientists recognized a verifiable *rara avis*, and dubbed it Cadborosaurus (The Cadboro Bay Lizard).

Mystical Significance

Dozens (at least) of water beasts virtually identical to the Cadborosaurus have been seen from ancient times to the present day. They appear throughout North America and virtually around the world, and their eyewitness accounts are given by persons of often impeccable credibility. The generally high level of reliability associated with these reports, together with the international scope of the phenomenon repeated with remarkable consistency over the course of centuries, make accusations that the matter is a deliberate hoax unlikely, if not impossible.

Yet, trying to establish the existence of Cadborosaurus and its ilk is similar to arguing a *habeas corpus* case. For all the excellent testimony, no physical remains of the creatures have ever been recovered and even the best photographs purporting to show the creature are dubious, at best.

Like the UFO phenomenon, many people are indeed seeing something real, even though material evidence is lacking.

The various Native American tribes which have occupied the Victoria area for past generations knew about the monster of Cadboro Bay long before the arrival of modern Europeans. Major Langley may have made the first documented sighting, but he was preceded by indigenous mythic traditions which described the same beast from deeply prehistoric times. These myths portray it as a transitory creature, able to swim between this and the Otherworld. The Indians still regard it as a thought-form, installed in the waters off Victoria unknown ages ago by a powerful shaman to protect the sacred character of the island.

A closely related variation of the same tradition depicts the monstrous thought-form as a nature-spirit, the visible expression of planetary energy or those not yet entirely understood forces within the Earth which effect human consciousness. A sacred site's concentrated earth-power is believed to interface with receptive human consciousness in such a way that the localized energy will express itself in the mind of the observer as a materialized and animated creature, most often and appropriately serpentine in conformity with an energy pattern. Such an explanation satisfies both the numerous, veritable sightings of the Cadborosaurus and the absence of physical proof for the beast's existence. It does indeed exist, perhaps not in a material dimension, but in the primeval and more fundamental relationship between human consciousness and the forces of our planet.

Directions

From the Visitors' Information Office in downtown Victoria, take Cadboro Bay Road to Oak Bay Avenue east to Beach Drive, which skirts Oak Bay, through Uplands Park and around Cadboro Bay itself.

Information

Tourism Association of Vancouver Island, 30245 Bastion Square, Victoria, B.C. V8W 1T3; tel. (250) 382-3551; fax (250) 382-3523.

Source Notes

Willis, Archie, *Victoria Times*, 9 October, 1933.

Niagara Falls: Evening Review, 29 November, 1933.

Gardener, Ray, "Caddy, King of the Coast," *Maclean*, 15 June, 1950.

Mackal, Roy P., *Searching for Hidden Animals*, New York: Stubba House, 1970.

The Chilliwack Ghosts
Frank Joseph

Canada's most famous haunted house may still be seen on William Street North, in Chilliwack, B.C. It was the subject of a radio documentary (CKNW, Vancouver) in 1980, when the painting made by a former resident was exhibited for the first time.

The full-length, eight-by-five-foot portrait is reportedly the image of an apparition occasionally encountered near the large bedroom window that faces out toward the street. Rendered in an unnatural mix of black and orange pigments, it shows a forlorn young woman, her face half obscured in shadow, her arms folded across her chest. The painting is the work of Hetty Frederickson. With her husband, Douglas, the Dutch-born artist moved to the William Street address before Christmas, 1965. The two-story structure was originally built in 1937, and is still referred to as the Frederickson house, even though the couple left in 1966 and were not the original owners. Doubtless, Hetty's painting associated her name with the residence ever since the piece was publicly shown.

The paranormal events they experienced there eventually forced them to move to Vancouver Island. From their first weeks at the Chilliwack house, husband and wife were plagued by extraordinary nightmares of remarkably similar content. The frightening dreams usually included a woman in a red dress patterned with yellow flowers. She appeared lying in the attic floor on her back, her face a mask of the most awful fear. Their recurrent nightmares were punctuated by daytime occurrences which were no less unnerving. An old bedstead that belonged to the original owners suddenly bumped across the floor under its own power. Dresser drawers abruptly opened, then angrily slammed shut. Doors banged suddenly on their hinges, as though propelled by invisible hands. The couple noticed a kind of cold spot in a darkened hallway. Standing there, they felt a malicious presence that raised the hairs on the back of their necks.

The disturbances climaxed the following May, when Hetty observed a mist appear near the bedroom window. The apparition gradually took form in the image of their nightmares. It was the same woman they remembered from their awful dreams. The following spring, the Fredericksons learned from a previous occupant that in 1954 a man residing at the house had murdered his wife, whose body he cemented into the chimney. Eventually overcome with guilt, he killed himself, leaving behind a suicide note that explained his crime. Hetty and Douglas were now convinced that the unnatural disturbances were results of a murder-suicide. These gruesome details were somehow discovered by the local press, which published a feature article about the haunting. The next day, a crowd of more than 700 curiosity seekers descended on the old house. Faced with the glare of unwelcome publicity from without and the ghostly activities within, the Fredericksons fled Chilliwack, never to return.

They moved to Vancouver Island, but even there something of Chilliwack haunted them, especially Hetty. Settling in Sayward, along the northeast coast of the island, Hetty began painting strange faces on slabs of cedar, using the natural wood grain as a base for each image. They were the faces of unknown persons, but their portraits were so individualized and their variety so great, they appeared to represent actual people. Creating the weird paintings became an obsession, so much so, Hetty began mass-producing them, not for sale, but to adorn the trail leading through a forested area north of the Campbell River.

The Valley of a Thousand Faces eventually grew into a strange tourist attraction, with visitors strolling among the pines, through which the sometimes disconcerting visage of a peculiar figure would peer with unsettling intensity. In truth, there were far more than the thousand images mentioned in the valley's name; before her death in 1993, Hetty completed in excess of 1,400 paintings on wood. Unfortunately, The Valley of a Thousand Faces closed shortly thereafter, and her unusual art work was distributed piecemeal among family and friends. Who were the persons she so vividly depicted in her paintings? What drove her to create such a large collection? Was she endeavoring to create portraits of the ghostly images who continued to haunt her, even after she left the Chilliwack house?

For two years, the house was abandoned. Then, in 1968, it was rented for four years by a group of musicians. What, if anything, they experienced they never shared with others. The house was purchased in 1972 by a family, whose members reported virtually identical phenomena encountered by the Fredericksons. Their dog, previously a sedate cocker spaniel, lived in a state of almost constant panic, and stubbornly refused to enter certain parts of the house, such as the hallway with its frightening cold spot. Within a year, this family, too, moved out. Since then, owners have come and gone, all with their stories of spectral appearances, nightmares and unexplainable kinetic activities, usually involving furniture and doors.

Today, the Frederickson house is unoccupied, its future as uncertain as its past.

Mystical Significance

A general consensus among investigators of the paranormal describes the Chilliwack ghosts as the energy residue of human will. Just as a sacred site is created by psychical forces interacting with a specific environment, so a haunting results when human trauma similarly impacts and alters the immediate surroundings wherein the trauma occurred. According to this theory, the apparitions seen at places like the Frederickson house are actually episodes of energy transference between living persons and the on-going vibrations still resonating at the site of their occurrence.

Still others believe more traditional explanations, which characterize such unusual activities as the struggles of the spirits of deceased persons prevented from "going on," and confined to a specific location by the extraordinary circumstances of their deaths. Whichever theory one may choose, places like the Frederickson house, while concentrations of undeniable spiritual energy, are not sacred sites. They have not been deliberately hallowed to any ennobling purpose. They are created by accident or fate and not intentionally developed through the practices of geomancy or other means to bring about a place of spiritual power.

So-called haunted establishments are almost invariably concentrations of negative or misguided energy of no immediate benefit for the living. Still, they are not entirely without merit. It is not necessary, much less recommended, for anyone to spend a night at the Frederickson house to appreciate the site's Otherworldly power. Seeing it from the outside is quite sufficient. Encounters such as these, even at a distance, may be useful, because the field of spiritual energy could be intense enough to touch the receptivity of an observer.

While meetings of this kind may certainly be unnerving, even at a distance, they nevertheless make it possible for the individual to feel his soul, as it were, thereby convincing ourselves of its reality on a profound level of knowing.

Directions

Chilliwack is located twenty-five miles (40 km) east of Abbotsford on Highway 1, sixty-four miles (103 km) east of Vancouver. Take Exit 116 or 119.

Information

Tourism Chilliwack, 44150 Luckakuck Way, Sardis, B.C. V2R 1A9; tel. 1-800-567-9535.

Source Notes

Lightbody, Mark and Tom Smallman. *Canada, a Travel Survival Kit*, Berkeley, CA.: Lonely Planet Publications, 1992.

Hervey, Sheila. *Some Canadian Ghosts*, Toronto: Simon & Schuster of Canada, 1973, p. 653.

The Christina Lake Pictograph
Frank Joseph

A pictograph is an illustrated symbol representing a certain idea. Thousands were painted, drawn or etched by prehistoric artists across North America. They appear to signify religious concepts or actual/mythical events. Among the largest and most mystifying examples of its kind, a 28-by-32-inch image (72 x 80 cm), appears on the wall of a grotto above Christina Lake, east of the Midway Mountains and about seventy-five miles (125 km) southeast of Kelowna.

Painted in a reddish orange ochre pigment, its outer illustrations are partially overgrown with calcite, an indication that the art work is very old. It depicts a colored, filled-in circle or large dot at the center of a bigger circle with a broad band extending horizontally from either side. A pair of thin, leglike lines fall vertically from the bottom of the circle, while a shorter pair of somewhat elongated deltoids sprout from the top. Two stick-figures apparently representing men stand at both sides of the leglike lines. The somewhat obscured elements next to them were probably two more stick-men. Of all the surviving Native American imagery known, nothing begins to resemble the Christina Lake find. It was credited to the Interior Salish, although the Indians never claimed it as their own, nor do they recognize the nature of its significance. The last Salish rock art was painted in the middle of the nineteenth century, and the grotto pictograph, as mentioned above, predates the modern era by many centuries.

The enigmatic design may nevertheless attempt to abstractly depict an old tale known among various tribes in the region. The story tells of a beautiful boy who fell from the nearby cliff into the water and was never seen again. Some versions portray him as the victim of wicked spirits, while others claim his fair looks won the heart of a goddess who dwells in a marvelous village at the bottom of the lake, where he lives with her in eternal bliss. Additional pictographs in the immediate vicinity are believed to exemplify various aspects of the legend and/or serve as warnings to stay away from the site.

Some modern interpreters of the Lake Christina pictograph believe it depicts an alien spacecraft descending from the sky. Human figures were included to provide scale, the UFOlogists argue.

The lake is beautiful, however rocky its shoreline, and the grotto is relatively accessible. No accompanying artifacts or physical evidence of ceremonial human habitation have been recovered from its interior.

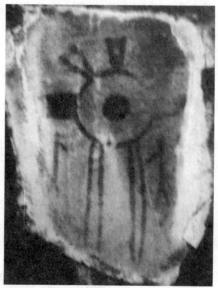

Christina Lake petroglyph.
Photo courtesy of Dennis Graf.

50

Mystical Significance

The Lake Christina pictograph would be extraordinary enough for its size, stylistic execution and intriguing design. But its setting clearly defines it as a sacred site of particular power. Beginning 20,000 and more years ago, grottoes or caves were centers of the most profound rituals acted on behalf of mystery religions honoring the Earth Mother. They were revered with deep awe as the womb and tomb of life. Initiations within their bowels almost invariably centered around the concept of death as the prelude to rebirth. It was here, in the natural sacred precinct of the Earth Mother Goddess herself, that her energies were deliberately encountered for life-transforming experiences. From the Cro-Magnon caverns of Lascaux to the modern Grotto of Our Lady at Lourdes, the feminine spirituality of our planet has been honored.

It would appear, then, that the pre-Salish pictograph portrays, not a flying saucer from outer space, but the Earth Mother, in whose natural shrine the art work was deliberately installed. She is represented by the circle with the large dot at the center, the eternally fertile (i.e., abundant) Navel of the World. The lines extending from the circle are her energies, toward which the human stick-figures extend their hands in order to empower themselves with her life-giving, life-enhancing forces. This interpretation is underscored by surviving Native American myths of the boy who fell into Christina Lake and was welcomed into eternal life by the goddess of a splendid kingdom far beneath the waves. The mythic elements of youth, death and rebirth at the hands of a nature-goddess at Christina Lake redefine the grotto as a wonderful sacred site of the kind found mostly in Europe. Sacred caves were far rarer in North America.

The British Columbian location could be something of an exception, since ancient residents may have detected particularly obvious (because strong) telluric forces in the grotto that attracted ritual attention. Nor was such attention the result of primitive religions or savage superstition. Some caverns or grottoes are known to emit high, concentrated levels of negative ions, which produce feelings of euphoria, well-being, spirituality and even artistic inspiration in human beings. The pictograph at Christina Lake would appear to be a lasting result of that negative-ion induced inspiration. If so, then it is a sign-post welcoming us from the deep past to partake of the Earth Mother energies still at work within the sacred grotto.

Directions

From Castlegar, take Highway 3 west thirty miles (49 km). Follow signs to Christina Lake.

Information

Christina Lake Tourist Association, Box 591, Christina Lake, B.C. V0H 1E0; tel. (250) 447-6161; fax (250) 447-6286.

Source Notes

Clark, Ella Elizabeth. *Indian Legends of Canada*, Toronto: McClelland & Stewart, 1960.

The Keremeos Mound
Frank Joseph

In a peaceful, largely unvisited area of British Columbia not far from the town of Keremeos, stands an earthen mound unique in all North America for the story associated with it. Today, it is a low, grassy earthwork in the valley of the Similkameen River. Visually, there is not much to attract attention, and, unless the visitor knows something about the legend of this physically unspectacular mound, one might move on without taking much notice. But it is the folk memory of the local Native people that imparts the simple structure with a unique character all its own.

The Similkameen people recall that one autumn day, long before the English or French arrived in Canada, a large group of bearded, white-faced strangers dressed in metal uniforms arrived from somewhere in the south. A battle soon erupted, during which many Indians were slain and some taken prisoner to be used as porters. The invaders with their new slaves marched northeast into the valley, proceeded around Okanagan Lake, and established their quarters at what is now the north end of Kelowna. The strangers were spied upon from a safe distance during the bitter winter, which depleted their numbers.

In spring, the remaining foreigners attempted to leave via the same route by which they had come, and set up temporary camp on a flat hill at

The Keremeos Mound.   *Photo by David Bornus.*

the edge of the Keremeos Valley. Later, on their way along the creek, they were set upon by large numbers of Similkameen warriors. While the alien soldiers fought desperately, killing many of the foe, they were at last overwhelmed by sheer weight of numbers. None of the mysterious whites survived. But the Indians were so impressed by the death-defying courage of their out-numbered enemy, all the fallen invaders were honorably entombed in an earthen mound, together with their armor and weapons. And there they still lie, within the clay embrace of the Keremeos Mound.

Mystical Significance

The Keremeos Mound myth is certainly valid, if only because it continues to endure in the folk tradition of the Similkameen people. It is not a fable to teach morality, nor a religious legend to preach reverence to the gods, but a historical myth that preserves some actual event of importance to subsequent generations of the tribe which experienced it. Beyond its historical validity, the identity of the white soldiers with beards and the time in which the bloody confrontation took place are uncertain.

Some investigators believe they were sixteenth-century Spaniards, and point to the "metal uniforms" remembered by the Indians. Two hundred years later, Spanish ships did indeed founder near the mouth of the Columbia River, and petroglyphs decorating a Keremeos Creek boulder known as the "Prisoner Paintings" portray what appear to be captives roped together by riders on horseback. But the meticulous expeditionary records of Imperial Spain do not list any royal enterprise to British Columbia.

Partial excavation of the Keremeos Mound did indeed yield breast plates and armor, but they were copper, a mineral not used by the Conquistadors, whose breast plates were made of steel. Copper armor was used, not by seventeenth-century Europeans, but by Bronze Age warriors of Troy, Greece, Egypt and all the high civilizations of the Ancient World from Ireland to Asia Minor. David Hatcher Childress, President of the World Explorers Club, wrote of a Haida Indian tour guide at Victoria's Royal British Columbia Museum, who "told us of how at the famous potlatch ceremonies, where a chief would make lavish gifts to his guests, thereby indebting them to him, the greatest gift that they could give was a piece of copper armor plating. The Haidas' most prized possessions were the ancient breast plates of copper handed down through the centuries. At important potlatch feasts, they would break off a piece of copper from one of the breast plates and offer it to an important guest."

Northeast of Kelowna, at Mill Creek, the rotten remains of a wooden structure was unearthed at a site associated with the white strangers' winter headquarters. The 1863 discovery seemed to confirm a Spanish identity after investigators determined that its logs had been cut by iron tools. Since then, archaeologists have learned that various peoples, thousands of years before the Spaniards, were using iron axes.

While the materials detailed in any mythic tradition may be often surprisingly accurate, trying to date an historical event preserved in myth is difficult, because our time frame is radically different than that of a less technologically sophisticated people, to whom time is, in any case, cyclical rather than linear. There is the additional problem of the myth itself, which has the Indians raising a burial mound for their enemies, whose armor and weapons were respectfully interred in the earthwork. The Native Americans never built mounds for their foes, and they certainly would not have buried superior weapons and armor along with them. Moreover, mound-building in Canada ended around 1400, long before any Spaniard could have possibly arrived in British Columbia. None of these historical facts render the Similkameen tradition untrustworthy, but instead push it back to a time preceding the Spanish by several millennia.

The Spanish identity of the bearded white men is further diminished by the myth's total absence of any reference to firearms or horses ("Prisoner Paintings" boulder to the contrary), elements which would have been undoubtedly given priority in the retelling, had they been encountered. To find out who really lies within the mound, we should listen to the other Native American traditions of the "Marine Men," likewise white, who arrived in great canoes from "a big lodge across the Sunrise Sea," to mine an astounding half a billion pounds of high grade copper from 3000 to 1200 B.C. For much of that prehistoric period, so the legends go, the Indians' ancestors and the Marine Men worked together in peace to satisfy the white strangers' hunger for the shiny metal, with which they decorated themselves. In fact, a place known as Copper Mountain, where large deposits of the mineral were worked from prehistoric times, lies only thirty-two miles (50 km) from Keremeos. Native Americans would have interred the bodies of these copper-obsessed foreigners, their friends for generations, with respect. The same legends go on to say that their friendship eventually soured into warfare. Perhaps the Similkameen myth is an amalgam of historical truths from the deep past. In any case, an ancient European Bronze Age identity for the strangers seems more applicable than any Spanish interpretation.

Serious excavation of the Keremeos Mound has yet to be undertaken by qualified investigators. If and when professionals have an opportunity to sift through its interior, circumstantial evidence and myth may be turned into archaeological fact. Today, visitors to the mound experience its aura as a genuine sacred site. They feel its dynamism undimmed by time. More than a burial structure, however historically thrilling, the location for its construction was chosen for the earth-energies detected at this specific place by the shaman, or tribal psychic, who determined such things. By heaping the soil up into a dome or breast-shape, the shaman was focusing the telluric power, concentrating and directing it for spiritual empowerment. It was this deliberate accumulating of planetary energy in the earthwork that went into the creation of every Indian mound. Those energies are still at work in the Keremeos structure.

Indeed, the area surrounding the mound is intensely alive with telluric power, most particularly at Keremeos Columns Provincial Park. Here, visitors behold a cliff of hexagonal basalt columns rising ninety meters high from a lava base. The Otherworldly effect of the gigantic columns twisted with the power of the Earth speaks to something unutterable and fundamental in our spirit.

Directions

Keremeos is eighteen miles (29 km) east of Hedley on Highway 3, forty-two miles (67 km) west of Princeton.

Information

Keremeos & District Chamber of Commerce; tel. (250) 498-6321.

Source Notes

Berton, Pierre. *The Mysterious North*, Toronto: McClelland & Stewart, 1956.

Barlee, N. L. *Gold Creeks and Ghosts Towns*, Toronto, Ontario: Hancock House Publishers, 1970.

Casgrain, Henri-Raymond. *Legends canadiens*, Quebec: Impr. A. Cote & Cie., 1876.

Kispiox
Frank Joseph

"Between the Banks" is an authentic Gitksan Indian village, known in the native language as 'Ksan. Its mountainous setting is dramatic in the extreme for this archaeologically correct recreation of an indigenous community with roots in the deeply prehistoric past. There are guided tours which are as informative as they are entertaining.

But for those hoping to find something less structured and more spiritual, 'Ksan should serve as a necessary prelude to another and nearby Gitksan village. Kispiox has a population of some 500 persons descended from the original Frog, Wolf and Fireweed Clans. The Frog was long ago well-respected by tribes down the Pacific coast as far as the southern California Chumash Indians for the number of shamans this clan produced. Surviving Chumash rock art brilliantly portrayed the shamanistic Frog in vibrant cave paintings of red, white, black and yellow. The Wolf preserve the tribal tradition of the Great Flood, from which all Native Americans trace their ancestry.

Inherently friendly, the people of Kispiox live their lives in the manner of their forbearers without the assistance of anthropologists. Visitors may see them perform their ceremonial dances or hear them chant their traditional songs unaffectedly and naturally. There are many gifted carvers among the Gitksan, as evidenced by their intricately crafted miniature sculpture in wood, stone and ivory of whales, bears, birds and turtles. But it is in the massive, awesome totem poles that their art reaches its highest levels of achievement. Fifteen cedar examples are grouped together in a sacred site near the confluence of the Skeena and Kispiox Rivers. While some of the poles have been recently made, others were erected long ago. In fact, the oldest totem pole in North America stands at a related village, Kitwancool, not far from Kispiox.

Mystical Significance

Cultural differences are not intrinsically wrong or evil. They define a people's identity and are an outgrowth of its folkish soul over the course of centuries and millennia. It stands to reason, then, that outsiders cannot become Indians for a day when visiting places like Kispiox, any more than the Gitksan can allow themselves to be totally absorbed into the modern world without sacrificing their fundamental identity. There is, nevertheless, a universal spiritual need in human beings. Culture is a particular people's response to that essential need.

With a properly balanced mind-set, visitors of various cultural backgrounds to Kispiox may appreciate and even derive inspiration from the ceremonial dances and chants of the Gitksan, without knowing every ritual detail and nuance. If we listen to the primal core of the music, its cadences and rhythmic inflections, we actually pierce the heart of its mystery and understand it on levels more sublime than narrow intellect. For anyone who wants his time spent at Kispiox to be something more meaningful than an anthropological entertainment, appreciating Gitksan is rich cultural overlay but harkening to the universal spirituality beneath it will bring the kind of significant experience through personal insight and discovery too often lacking in contemporary society.

The sacred site focus of Kispiox is its concentration of totem poles where the two rivers come together. By no means haphazardly chosen, their collective position was established by Native principles of geomancy, that ancient science of interpreting the landscape in spiritual terms, to harmoniously fit human habitation into the natural scene. The totem poles comprise a haunted place, filled with unseen energies and a ghostly presence. Their age, spanning ancient and modern times, preserves the living continuity of spiritual heritage from prehistoric generations to the present.

That spirituality is personified in the mostly zoomorphic images which rise upon the wooden obelisks. Walking among them and allowing their peculiar resonance to penetrate our conscious and unconscious mind is to empower ourselves for the tasks laid out by our destiny. Such an appreciation of Kispiox simultaneously broadens and deepens our awareness, and hence, appreciation of the world.

Representation of a shaman chief from the Pacific Northwest. Los Angeles Natural History Museum, California. *Photo by William Donato.*

Directions

Kispiox lies sixteen miles (26 km) north of Hazelton, off Highway 16.

Information

North by Northwest Tourism Association of British Columbia, Box 1030 (NW) Smithers, B.C. V0J 2N0; tel. 1-800-663-8843.

Source Notes

Colin, Paul. *Native American Art and Society*, New York: Brown-MacMillan, 1966.

Krueger, Ruth. *Shaman Symbolism*, Chicago: Anthropomorphic Publishers Inc., 1990.

Oak Bay's Ghost Conference

Frank Joseph

One of the best-documented, regular ghost sightings is also among the most unusual. Every year, a conference of apparitions materializes at the southern end of Vancouver Island. Near the Strait of Georgia, sprawls the Victoria Golf Course, not far from the venerable Victoria Hotel. Sometimes the spectral convocation meets on the lawn of the hotel itself, more often along a rugged spit of land thrusting into Oak Bay.

Long-time residents of the area have been familiar with the unearthly meetings since 1936. It was in that Depression year that tragic human events set in motion a persistent, albeit supernatural, phenomenon difficult to explain. The story begins with a formerly wealthy Victoria investor, who gradually lost his fortune during the economic chaos that followed the "crash" of 1929. As his financial assets dwindled away, he took to drink, so much so, his lovely wife, no longer able to cope with his bouts of physical abuse, decided to divorce her troubled and troubling husband. Her announcement stung him like the worst personal betrayal, and, in a paroxysm of drunken rage, he strangled her to death at a place near the present golf course. When he eventually regained his sobriety, he was overwhelmed with grief and drowned himself in a nearby pond.

Very shortly thereafter the apparitions were first noticed by local Victorians all too familiar with the murder. Since then, the group of mistlike human shapes have been seen virtually every year since. Only the female figure is usually identified as belonging to the strangled wife. Who the others may be, no one has been able to determine. Usually, she stands mournfully apart from them. Her murderous husband is either absent or lost among the group of strangers, whose numbers always vary because they are indefinite, although the shadowy crowd is said to number no more than half a dozen persons.

Their annual reunion takes place in the spring, although on no set date.

They have been observed to meet in early April some years or late May in others. They shimmer into half-existence for hardly more than a minute or two, then vanish for another twelve months. Witnesses sometimes report hearing whispering voices along the shoreline immediately before, during or shortly after the phantoms appear. Apparently more than local fable, as many as seven witnesses at a time have seen the lone lady and her stand-offish companions. The phenomenon, while frequent, is not as regular as clockwork, and has gone unreported some years. Occasional attempts at astral communication have so far failed, in that the ghosts seem oblivious to the living.

Likewise, efforts at photographing the event do not validate the numerous oral reports collected over the last several decades. However, a recording made during a good sighting in 1991 did evidence hushed, unintelligible voices not associated with activity taking place in the area. Acoustic researchers investigating the cassette tape recording used digital back-tracking instruments to isolate a faint background noise not audible within the spectrum of human hearing. During their first play-back of the sub-sound recording, they were amazed to hear the strains of a dance band popular in the mid-1930s.

Mystical Significance

Researchers of the paranormal generally concur that a haunting of the kind demonstrated at Oak Bay represents a spiritual endless loop. Some deeply traumatic act initiates a recurring residue of the forces which set it in motion. These forces overlap from their dimension into our own when a vortex of time pulls them into a visible level of existence.

It is possible at such moments to actually glimpse that nexus connecting our present reality with the Otherworld of timelessness. What observers see at such moments is the accumulation of energies taking the form of an originating event which transcended both spheres of being. In the Oak Bay case, the identity of the lone female figure is associated with the spirit of the murdered wife. The presence and identity of the other figures, however, are entirely enigmatic. Although the Oak Bay phenomenon is somewhat unique for its number of persons, the circumstances which brought it about are remarkably similar to the Frederickson haunting in Chilliwack, described earlier. There, as well, the murder of a wife by her suicidal husband began a powerful haunting. Investigators believe, too, that the thousands of portraits on wood Hetty Frederickson painted during her lifetime were depictions of a large number of apparitions she encountered at the Chilliwack house. The recurrence of such phenomena renders the areas in which they manifest themselves true sacred sites, in that they create a temporary link when our material dimension and the Otherworld interface.

Linkages like these are important, regardless of the circumstances which brought them about, because they convince us on our most profound level of a spiritual realm beyond our own, but inextricably connected to it. Such inner comprehension and recognition is the fundamental basis for all personal spiritual development, the catharsis or born again experience from which the human soul grows toward the totality of its full potential.

Information

Tourism Victoria's Travel Info Center, 812 Wharf St.; tel. (250) 382-2127.

Source Notes

Branden, Victoria. *Understanding Ghosts*, London: Victor Gollancz, Ltd., 1980.

Creighton, Helen. *Bluenose Ghosts*, Toronto: The Ryerson Press, Ltd., 1968.

The Man Who Fell from Heaven
Frank Joseph

The old story was told by Coast Tsimshian Indians of the man who fell from Heaven, and left proof of his fall at an unusual rock. They said he was a great chief who was an even greater shaman, because he conjured unseen forces at his command. As an example of his powers, he once went into a deep trance, then slowly levitated his body from the ground. He continued to gradually ascend until he was entirely lost to view above the clouds. Several days later, the shaman was seen falling from the sky, and he landed flat on his back onto a slab of rock. He survived the experience without a scratch, and, when he arose from his landing spot, observers were amazed to see the outline of their chief pressed into the face of the rock. His name was Metlakatla, which in the coastal Tsimshian dialect means "him from across the water." It may signify his overseas origins, perhaps among the Pacific Northwest's islands, some of which are still revered as sacred.

Today, as though in confirmation of the Native American legend, visitors to the Tsimshian Reservation may see the man-sized carving of the Metlakatla figure, an anthropomorphic image cut into the almost smooth surface of a roughly rectangular rock out-cropping. Although other man-mounds may be found across the southern regions of Canada, the Metlakatla feature is unique as the only intaglio of its kind. In its vicinity some forty different archaeological sites have been identified. More than half (twenty-seven) are shell middens, or piles of food remains left by prehistoric villagers. There are also more than a dozen groups of petroglyphs nearby.

On-going research reveals an ever-deepening antiquity to the Venn Passage, in which the images and mounds are located. Interestingly, they date back to the late fourth millennium B.C., a period coinciding with the sudden beginnings of cultural florescence in other parts of the world, from Japan to Egypt.

Mystical Significance

Stories of human levitation abound in folk traditions throughout the world. They are invariably associated with deep-trance states and generally regarded as proof of great spiritual attainment. Interestingly, persons who use breath meditation to reach profound levels of introspection often experience the sensation of flight. As they count their breaths from one to seven, they feel as though they are rising. Counting back down from seven to one, the feeling is akin to descent. Adepts believe these sensations are nothing less than the rise and fall of the soul in altered consciousness.

The Tsimshian account of the man who fell from Heaven is hardly more than a fairy tale if accepted only at face value. But regarded as a spiritual allegory, it defines the Metlakatla intaglio as a sacred site used by persons on a vision-quest to reach high levels of meditation. Moreover, investigators believe the crystalline matrix of the rock itself, together with

Photo by Nancy Robertson, courtesy of The Daily News, Prince Rupert, B.C.

its location at or near an earthquake fault zone, possesses special qualities which greatly facilitate altered states of consciousness.

Their conclusions are no idle speculation. Laboratory studies at the University of California (Berkeley) have demonstrated that the bio-electric circuitry of the human mind will interface with subtle electrical fields in the Earth set up when seismic forces exert pressure on quartz crystal. Effects include feelings of physical buoyancy, inner serenity and spiritual insight. Persons seeking meditation reclined in the indentation, their vision-quest boosted by ingesting mild narcotics and, more importantly, through a receptive mind.

Directions

The Metlakatla man intaglio is located on the southwestern tip of Robinson Point in Prince Rupert, 447 miles (721 km) west of Prince George on Highway 16. The area is served by B.C. Ferries from Prince Rupert to Skidegate (Queen Charlotte Islands), ninety-two miles (149 km) by sea, with an eight-hour cruising time.

Information

Prince Rupert Travel Info Center, 1st Avenue & McBride Street, Box 669, Prince Rupert, B.C., V8J 3S1; tel. (250) 624-5637; fax (250) 627-8009.

Source Notes

Clark, Ella Elizabeth. *Indian Legends of Canada*, Toronto: McClelland & Stewart, 1960.

Fowke, Edith. *Folklore of Canada*, Toronto: McClelland & Stewart, 1976.

Nimpkish
Frank Joseph

Islands are traditional settings for sacred sites, and Cormorant Island, in Alert Bay, off the eastern shores of north Vancouver Island, is no exception. What makes Cormorant special is the high level of preservation that surrounds Native American religious artifacts and the endurance of ancient belief systems by the people who continue to venerate a primeval spirituality. Fully half of the residents are Kwakiutl Natives. Their island acts as a successful refuge against the destructive inroads of modern materialism, thereby ensuring the continuance of nature-worship traditions extending back over the millennia.

Thus allowed to flourish, these age-old traditions, rooted deeply in the very soil of Cormorant Island, are more than preserved—they continue to develop. In this relatively pristine cultural environment, the world's largest totem pole stands as testimony to the spiritual growth that continues to blossom here. It has grown so tall because the Kwakiutl went undiscovered by zealous missionaries, who always condemned and sometimes pulled down all physical expressions of the Old Religion. The Nimpkish totem pole was gradually added to over the generations, until its present height renders all further additions virtually impossible. Tribal elders decided long ago that no more changes to the art work would be made. The pole is nothing less than awe-inspiring, as much for its extraordinary size as its self-evident craftsmanship.

The colorful skill of its carvings is in perfect proportion to its imposing height. The Nimpkish pole is not especially old. None are particularly venerable, owing to their cedar construction in a wet environment, where moisture rots even the most painted or laminated examples. The average totem pole cannot survive much more than a century, save those near the Yukon, where the air is far more dry. Although the base of the Nimpkish pole is believed to have been created sometime in the early 1800s, the structure's final touches were accomplished before 1950.

Beyond the 120 foot (37 m) high structure, visitors pass over a boardwalk to an ecological preserve, Gator Gardens, where cedar, hemlock and pine trees hung with great broadlooms of moss rise in ghostly fashion from a black-water swamp. Watching from the branches are observant ravens and lordly eagles. Nearby is the Nimpkish sacred burial ground, a mix of Christian and Native symbols among the grave markers.

Close-up of Nimpkish totem pole details.
Photo courtesy of William Donato.

Mystical Significance

The term "totem pole" is a common misnomer. None of the numerous figures, nor even the pole itself, are objects of worship. Instead, they signify the lineage of the tribe or tribal chieftain who erected the pole. As such, they are primarily memorial or heraldic devices to at once proclaim the historico-mythic identity of a people and their leaders. But they represent more than a kind of vertical family crest. The poles relate often intricate legends and spiritual beliefs in dramatic, visual metaphors among the images of fantastic animals and anthropomorphic shapes.

They are not necessarily read from top to bottom, nor from bottom to top. While tribal elders are possessed of the symbolic meanings attached to all elements incorporated into the carvings, such knowledge is not required for observers to fundamentally grasp the power of the pole in its entirety. In essence, the Nimpkish totem pole dramatically announces the powerful sacred character of Cormorant Island, where all the mysterious forces of Nature gather to create a divine vortex, of which the Kwakiutl are the honored stewards. The great pole emanates various meanings. It is the phallic *axis mundi*, the symbol of perpetual abundance and ever-up-welling fertility around which the world revolves. The Nimpkish pillar also speaks of the Kwakiutls' ancestral home, a far greater island across the Pacific Ocean. Long, long ago, their forefathers left their holy isle, besieged by fire and flood, to resettle on little Cormorant, where they recreated a scaled-down version of their blessed isle lost beneath the waves of the western island.

Even visitors unacquainted with all the particulars of this ancestral myth may intuit the significance of the Nimpkish pole for its immanent power. If the sensation of mystery is the precondition for opening one's heart and mind to the potential of a sacred site, then the great totem pole of Cormorant Island amply achieves its purpose. The very wood from which it was made is holy, because cedar is universally regarded among Native American tribes as fragrant to the gods. It, too, is a sacred element. The pole's placement within the ritual context of the numinous swamp and the closeby burial ground defines the physical and mystical parameters of the sacred center, the spiritual heart of the island.

Gator Gardens rises with the holy cedar, together with hemlock, symbolic of the dissolution of forms, and the pine of everlastingness. They stand serenely among the black-water swamp, and combine into an allegory for the reassurance of the soul's immortality rising from the waters of death. The presence of a burial ground in this symbolic arrangement of man and nature reaffirms the conquest of life.

Directions

Cormorant Island is accessible by regular ferries from Port McNeill and Sointula.

Information

Alert Bay Travel Info Center, 116 Fir Street, Box 28, Alert Bay, B.C., V0N 1A0; tel. (250) 974-5213; fax (250) 974-5470.

Tourism Information Center, PO Box 28, Alert Bay, B.C. V0N 1A0; tel. (250) 974-5213; fax, (250) 974-5470.

Source Notes

Borrows, Stanley. *Native American Village Sites of the U.S. and Canada*, Vermont: Eiler Publishers Inc., 1969.

Colin, Paul. *Native American Art and Society*, New York: Brown-MacMillan, 1966.

The Columneetza Stone
Frank Joseph

Today, Williams Lake is a peaceful mecca for fishermen who prize the quiet loveliness, as well as the big catches afforded by its picture-perfect waters. The lake is also a ranching and timber industry hub of the whole region, known as the Stampede Capital of British Columbia. It was not always so. In 1864, a bloody series of engagements was fought at its coast between the Native peoples and the European newcomers. In what history remembers as the Chilcotin Indian War, white homesteaders—women and children—were scalped, tortured, killed or taken prisoner. In retaliation, soldiers and volunteers massacred whole Indian villages without regard to the actual perpetrators.

From the midst of the escalating carnage arose a true man of peace, Willy'um, chief of the Shuswap tribe. His compassion for both sides and extraordinary diplomatic skills pacified the bellicose braves of his own people and the vindictive whites. It was primarily through his intervention that whole families of white settlers were spared horrible massacre. Out of sincere gratitude, the lake around whose shores the two peoples had endeavored to exterminate each other was re-christened and anglicized as Williams Lake. The far older Indian name for the same body of water was Columneetza, Athabascan for "meeting place of the Lordly people." Columneetza stood not so much for the Shuswaps as it did for the shamans of various tribes, which regarded the lake as a sacred center for meditation, vision-quests and psychic-spiritual exercises. It was the sacred character of the site which motivated Chief Willy'um, a devoted man, to make every effort on behalf of peace.

His successful effort was solemnicized at the absolute center of Columneetza's sacred site with a ritual stone. This was a beautiful omphalos, an *axis mundi*, the absolute midpoint of the energies brought into balance and harmony through his heroic efforts. The stone is a remarkable blend of alternating bands of white and purple quartzite. It was upon this sacred stone that peace was established in the area. And although subsequent generations of gold-hungry prospectors violated the spirit symbolized by the attractive stone in an orgy of greed and debauchery, it still stands as an enduring, natural monument to man's better instincts and the center of an eternally sacred site.

Mystical Significance

The Canadian omphalos is essentially the same as its more famous counterpart in Greece, the ancient sacred center of Delphi. Despite the virtually incessant conflicts which ravaged the Classical World, warring parties otherwise engaged in mutual slaughter put aside their weapons and their hatred when meeting at the Navel of the World above the Gulf of Corinth. A holy stone was at the absolute center of Delphi, just as as Chief Willy'um's ritual energies at Columneetza revolved around a solemnized stone. This Greek–Shuswap comparison is not made as an example of cultural contact, but to demonstrate an archetype of mankind's collective unconscious, as the pioneering Swiss psychologist, Carl Jung, defined such otherwise incomprehensible correspondences between peoples separated by vast distances and many thousands of years. The stone at Williams Lake may have been selected because of its alternating white and deep purple bands, signifying perhaps to the Shuswap shamans the white and Indian peoples.

Shaman's Regalia, the altered state of conciousness that merges the human soul into the underlying soul of nature through close identification with animal spirits. Display at the Vancouver Historical Museum.   *Photo by Frank Joseph.*

In the sacred stone, they were represented as harmoniously part of an object common to them both.

Even today, the Columneetza stone effects the contemplative observer as a kind of natural mandala to facilitate meditation and inner-tranquility. As such, it continues to serve as a meditative focal point for visitors who may use the attractive stone to reach those levels of inner and outer harmony fundamental for feelings of personal peace and reconciliation with our fellow creatures.

Directions

Williams Lake is located sixteen miles (25 km) north of 150 Mile House on Highway 97; 348 miles (540 km) north of Vancouver; 148 miles (238 km) south of Prince George.

Information

Williams Lake & District Travel Info Center, 1148 Broadway South, Highway 97 South, Williams Lake, B.C. V2G 1A2; tel. (250) 392-5025; fax (250) 392-4214.

Source Notes

Colin, Paul. *Native American Art and Society*, New York: Brown-MacMillan, 1966.

McVey, Kevin. *The Navel of the World*, San Francisco: Rutledge Publisher, 1987.

In the Realm of Stillness
Frank Joseph

As a steam freighter inched its way through the mist-shrouded darkness of the waters off the southern tip of Vancouver Island in the late
summer of 1889, the foghorn at Race Rocks sounded its warning
through the night. Although less than a fifth of a mile away from the
blast of recurring sound, those aboard the ship heard nothing, not
even the waves lapping against the side of their ship's hull, as the
vessel passed into what mariners knew and dreaded as "the region of
inaudibility," an acoustically dead zone of remarkable silence. Only
moments later, however, that ineffable stillness was shattered by the
horrendous noise of collision, as a ridge of rocks tore along a length
of keel, splintering timbers and opening the ship's bowels to the
greedy sea. In an instant of terror and chaos, the freighter hauled
over, her capsizing death-throes taking several dozen sailors to their
lightless graves beneath the water.

That turn-of-the-century wreck was not the first, nor by any means the
last victim claimed by a narrow area of sea, whose indefinite boundaries
encompass a sunken graveyard of doomed ships. The crews of vessels
which proceed into that watery arena of death report that all sound seems
muffled and substantially reduced; the air grows suddenly calm and the
usual cries of seabirds are not heard. The men aboard ship are not so much
frightened as they experience an inner serenity that appears to parallel the
inexplicable quiet into which they sail. But the strange peace they feel is
terribly misleading, because it is often a prelude to catastrophe.

While debunkers admit the so-called zone of silence is a real-enough
phenomena, they believe its causes are entirely natural, not supernatural.
A writer for the *Niagara Falls Evening Review* reported that scientific
opinion identified a large rock which, together with a nearby service
building, was responsible for blocking the sound of the foghorn. After
authorities raised the horn by an additional thirty feet to completely clear
the offending rock, no further mishaps in the channel separating the Strait
of Juan de Fuca from the Pacific Ocean are known to have taken place.

Other investigators point out, however, that vessels negotiating the
controversial passage no longer depend upon the foghorn, but use radar as
their chief navigational aid. And while serious accidents of the kind that

claimed so many ships and lives until the advent of electronic directional instruments in the mid-1950s do not occur there, sailors who venture across the seas off Race Rocks still occasionally experience an eerie calm that descends on the face of the waters. Neither wind nor any sounds from the shore may be heard under the invisible cover of an deadening silence. As the *Evening Review* reporter concluded, "Whatever the answer—an excuse for faulty navigation, a sound-shielding rock or an unnatural phenomenon—the legend persists."

Mystical Significance

Zones of silence, such as that encountered at Race Rocks, are common features of a sacred site. Visitors to Ohio's Great Serpent Mound or the Marching Bear Mounds of Iowa often report walking into an invisible precinct clearly defined by a profound serenity, as though a glass dome had descended over the location. Such arenas of quiet are invariably accompanied by heavy impressions of serenity and sanctity, as though visitors had entered a great cathedral.

The same stillness is known at Canada's Race Rocks. In the general area are other phenomena typical of a sacred site; namely, ghostly apparitions and sightings of a serpentine creature (see the Oak Bay Ghost Conference and the Cadborosaurus earlier). These manifestations are results of the Earth energies focused in a vortex at the south end of Vancouver Island. Such energies interface with the human brain's bio-electrical

The Realm of Stillness.   *Photo by Nancy Mostad.*

71

circuitry to produce (or induce) the effects reported by numerous witnesses over time.

It is the concentration of telluric forces which render the Race Rocks area a sacred site, because in places such as these we may tune in to the heartbeat of the Mother of us all—the Earth.

Directions

Race Rocks lies in the waters off the southern extremity of Vancouver Island, where a narrow channel separates the Pacific Ocean from the Strait of Juan de Fuca.

Information

Victoria Travel Info Center, 812 Wharf St., Victoria, B.C. V8W 1T3; tel. (250) 382-2127; fax (250) 382-6539.

Source Notes

Colombo, Robert. *Mysterious Canada*, Toronto: Doubleday Canada, 1988.

Randolf, Reginald. *Canadian Phenomena*, Toronto: Yorkshire Press Ltd., 1946.

The Miracle of Chemainus
Frank Joseph

As readers of this book may have suspected by now, the southeastern coasts of Vancouver Island comprise an extensive sacred site, a psychic precinct, wherein paranormal occurrences of various kinds continue to be encountered by eyewitnesses. And while we generally think of such arenas of the supernatural as part of some deeply prehistoric tradition, at least one example is an entirely modern phenomenon. It may be found in the small mill town of Chemainus, between the larger locations of Ladysmith in the north and Duncan in the south. Today, its citizens refer to it as "The Little Town that Did." Just what it did rendered the place a sacred site.

Chemainus was born from a sawmill that began attracting permanent workers in 1862. For the next one hundred years, its residents enjoyed moderate prosperity and came to love the inauspicious town. In 1982, however, the mill was shut down, a victim of the hard recession that wracked North America at the time, putting 400 workers on the streets. Chemainus went into decline. Civic pride sank, as the streets grew increasingly dingy and public parks and buildings began to fall into shameful disrepair. The townspeople's morale was low, and young people sought lives far from the homes of their families in other parts of the world. Chemainus was written off by most observers as a town doomed to inevitable extinction.

But strangely, defiantly, from the depths of despair for the future of their town, the citizens rallied in a last-ditch attempt to rescue themselves. The town that had for more than a hundred years depended entirely upon economic materialism sought salvation in art. Local artists were called upon to volunteer their talents for the sake of the common good. They painted a large, public mural that graphically depicted the calamity facing Chemainus. Stirred by the excellence of its representation, another mural portraying the history of the town appeared on another wall of some abandoned building. With this second and equally successful painting, an inertia among all the town's artists was felt, and soon murals displaying area culture and local characters began appearing everywhere. The painting became almost frenetic and spread from walls to litter bins and anything else that might even remotely serve as a canvas.

Not only the profusion, but the excellence of the art work revitalized the physical appearance of the town. The murals encompassed a broad variety of execution, from the clearly representational and lifelike to the fantastic and expressionistic, but mostly on a larger-than-life scale. If Chemainus was going to die, she would do so in style. But the town did not die. The flurry of artistic activity attracted the notice of other Vancouver Islanders, beyond to the mainland. The townspeople's dramatic efforts were showcased and praised by television and newspaper reporters and columnists. Soon, an unexpected influx of tourists converged on Chemainus, so much so shops and restaurants reopened. There were new craft stores and a tourism center was established. Even the sawmill reopened, as the town went beyond reclaiming its former economic status to become freshly prosperous.

At this writing, there are thirty-two murals in Chemainus, with more being executed, resulting in Canada's largest permanent outdoor art gallery. Among the most outstanding and consistently popular examples are

"Company Store" and "Chemainus Tugboat." To crown their success, the townspeople were awarded the prestigious first-place award in the New York downtown revitalization competition of 1983.

Mystical Significance

Typical characteristics of any sacred site are its powers of renewal, regeneration, revitalization. Whether revival is achieved through telluric forces focused by the Earth itself in special vortexes, by the agencies of shamanistic rituals hallowed by millennia or because of other, less dramatic energies mean nothing. All that matters is that some space of ground or water becomes sanctified to a spiritual purpose. The common will to civic survival was manifested by the people of Chemainus, whose energies concentrated themselves in the creation of art, an art that not only reflected their dilemma, but transcended it. For more than a century before, they and their fathers and grandfathers lived entirely on the materialistic level. When that level fell out from under their feet, they were

"Native Heritage"   *Paul Ygartua, 1983.*

forced to either fall with it or ascend to the next higher level of human endeavor, art. The aesthetic sense is, moreover, equivalent to our spiritual sense, because it is through the ennobling examples of art that spirituality manifests itself to us. The aesthetic sense is our bridge from physical representation to the ineffable powers of the soul.

On a communal level, the residents of Chemainus grasped the artistic link to spirituality. With it, they brought back their beloved town from

"Waiting for the Reindeer"   Sandy Clark, 1983.

otherwise certain death to a newer, more attractive life. Consequently, the ubiquitous murals transcend civic improvement or even art itself. They are assertions of the will to live, the human desire to defeat degeneracy and death by the powers which lay within their own community. The towns-people did not beg for help from outsiders. They sought within themselves for their own survival energies.

Their story was repeated in the United States, at a small community of North Carolina, where a country parish was saved at the last moment from financial destruction by an act of faith transposed into a similar artistic effort. Frescoes painted at St. Mary's Episcopal Church, in Glendale Springs, are parallel testimonials to a people's will to survive and evolve. These energies are likewise self-evident in The Little Town that Did, a modern sacred site to inspire and emulate.

Directions

Chemainus is located six miles (10 km) north of Crofton on Hwy 1A.

Forty-three miles (70 km) north of Victoria, eleven miles (17 km) north of Duncan.

Information

Chemainus Travel Info Center, 9758 Chemainus Road, Box 575, Chemainus, B.C. V0R 1K0; tel. (250) 246-3944; fax (250) 246-3251.
Arts & Business Council of Chemainus, PO Box 1311, Chemainus, B.C. V0R 1K0; tel. (250) 246-4701; fax (250) 246-3251

Source Notes

Scherver, Russell. *Modern Canada*, Washington, D.C.: National Geographic Society, 1989.

Wilhelm, Roger. *Social Art*, New York: Northrup Press Inc., 1995.

Thunderbird Park
Frank Joseph

A sacred site is sometimes created inadvertently, when various numinous elements are unintentionally brought together at a specific location. It was just such a undeliberate set of circumstances which resulted in a concentration of spiritual power behind Victoria's Royal British Columbia Provincial Museum. As part of their efforts to showcase local archaeology, the curators set aside a nearby park for a collection of totem poles from around the province. The location they chose was a small, secluded square of verdant landscape which perfectly set off the lofty and ancient art work. The work began in 1940, but an extensive renovation program from 1952 to 1955 resulted in the park as it is known today. It forms the finest group of totem poles in the world.

Intricately carved by Native sculptors of various Pacific Coast tribes, the wood monuments tower over visitors like an Otherworldly forest. The collection forms a perfect counterpart to the prehistoric art and artifacts on display in the museum. More significantly, Thunderbird Park has its own magical atmosphere generated by the gaunt totem poles leaning against the sky. The breezes which sometimes blow among their tops make them sigh or sing in haunting moans or snatches of windswept song. There are some fifty monuments altogether, the largest assembly of its kind in Canada, with new examples being erected, as some of the older poles are taken down for replacement or refurbishment.

While all of the totem poles are authentically Native American, none are older than seventy-five years, due to the nature of the medium in which they are carved. The pervading moisture of Victoria will eventually rot the wood over time, despite the best efforts at preservation. Actually, it is this process of decay and renewal that is central to the belief systems of tribal societies, because all matter and nonmatter (i.e., the human soul) are connected to the cyclical character of existence.

Mystical Significance

There are many mythic images represented among the totem poles behind the museum, but one dominates all the rest from its highest perch atop the monuments. This is the Thunderbird, from which the park's name is derived. The Thunderbird is no ordinary deity in the Native American pantheon. Its origins in deep antiquity hint of prehistoric contacts between the Pacific Northwest and other parts of the ancient world, even with the lost island civilizations of Mu and Atlantis.

The Thunderbird is so named after the claps of thunder produced by his flapping wings. Lightning flashes from his eyes and he is the bringer of rain, sometimes of floods. He first brought water to the Earth, from which the earliest vegetation grew. Interestingly, his concept extends all along the Pacific coasts of North America, from Alaska to southern California. He is also recognized along the

Thunderbird Park, B.C., petroglyphs.

Photo by Frank Joseph.

77

eastern shores of Asia, leading James Churchward, the leading authority on the sunken land of Mu, to conclude that veneration of the Thunderbird began in that vanished culture. Churchward's view is suggested by the Algonquian-speaking Indians, who refer to the Thunderbird as "our grandfather," a term for ancestor. Moreover, Thunderbird's myth tells of his frequent battles with evil powers deep beneath the ocean, another suggestive reference to sunken Mu.

But the primeval creature was also known to the ancient Greeks, who assigned the woodpecker identical qualities. They also identified it with warfare, as did the Native Americans. Several totem pole carvings of the Thunderbird in the Provincial Museum Park depict him with a face over his abdomen. This is a representation of the Navel of the World mystery religion supposedly originated in Atlantis, from which it spread over much of the world before that city's final destruction. The Navel cult's chief tenet was affirmation of the soul's reincarnation in a new earthly life after death. Easter Island, in the South Pacific, was known to its native inhabitants as *Rapa nui*, or the Navel of the World, after a religion of the same name was practiced and headquartered there. Indeed, Haida and other Indian shamans still regard the face on grandfather's navel as signifying the eternal womb of the universe. When so carved, the Thunderbird assumes the identity of the Oversoul, the triumph of spirit over the dissolution of material form.

Totem poles are allegories of myth frozen in art. And while the Thunderbird is the dominant character in these great pillars of carved wood, he is not the only revealing figure to appear. Another bird of seminal importance is Raven, the bringer of magic and healing, most associated with the shaman's art. He is sometimes accompanied by Eagle, another shaman symbol, the personification of the Great Spirit and the soaring connection between this and the Otherworld. Hawk also appears on the poles. He is the personification of power and the deliverer of omens (in Jungian terms, synchronicity or meaningful coincidence). Bear looks out from among his fellow beasts. He exemplifies the eternal rebirth of all things in his deathlike hibernation, from which he awakens each spring. Wolf is the teacher of life's survival lessons. He epitomizes instinct and cunning. Beaver is Earth energy, water energy, the clan and family. Frog is purification through water in all its powers, from ocean breakers to tears. But the supreme water symbol, and one of the greatest represented on the totem poles, is Whale, "he who remembers," the custodian of living memory, who still swims among the sunken, ancestral cities of Mu and

Atlantis, and who sings their old stories, as well as all the others which memorialize the past.

Visitors to Victoria's Thunderbird Park may be able to trace some of these mythic-metaphysical themes among the larger-than-life-size beings which glare down from their vertical heights. The poles are read from top to bottom. The images speak for themselves in the archetypes they exemplify and in the interpretation of our own spirit. Their collection in so attractive a park creates a genuine sacred site, where the old traditions find a new location to generate their timeless magic.

Directions

Thunderbird Park is in downtown Victoria, behind the Provincial Museum, on the corner of Belleville and Douglas Streets.

Information

Royal British Columbia Museum, 675 Belleview Street, Victoria, B.C. V8V 1X4; tel. (250) 387-2434; fax (250) 387-5360.

Source Notes

Clark, Ella Elizabeth. *Indian Legends of Canada*, Toronto: McClelland & Stewart, 1960.

Petroglyph Park
Frank Joseph

Vancouver Island is rich in paranormal phenomena, prehistoric and contemporary. A mass-haunting, sea serpent, zone of silence, totem pole park and more line its shores or inhabit its interior. A few miles south of Nanaimo, on the east coast of Vancouver Island, lies a genuine, once obscure and long-revered sacred site preserved as a public facility. Sitting alone off the main highway lies Petroglyph Provincial Park. Petroglyphs are symbolic images inscribed in stone. They do not constitute writing, although they most certainly convey specific meanings. Petroglyphs are among the oldest survivals of man's early attempts to perpetuate his ideas, events he experienced or beliefs he felt were essential.

While they are relatively common along the Pacific coasts, none are more ancient than those found here. They have been dated by archaeologists to at least 10,000 years ago, a time when the last Ice Age had just come to an end. The Vancouver Island examples, therefore, represent some of the oldest proof for humans in North America. Despite their extreme age, they are remarkably well preserved. It was only the numerous generations of Native peoples who venerated the incised images that ensured their continued existence. So too, their formerly remote location protected them from the ravages of Christian zealotry or ignorant vandalism in modern times. The petroglyphs are all the more vulnerable for the sandstone on which they appear. A marked trail to the park leads directly from a car lot and winds through a fragrant woods to the site.

The petroglyphs are remarkable not only for their profound antiquity, but they depict some images repeated infrequently if at all in other parts of coastal British Columbia. Among these curious figures various Native American shamans have identified the representation of an otherwise inexplicable beast known as the sea-wolf. Part killer whale and part wolf, it is believed to be the destructive spirit of the depths which devoured the great homeland across the Sunset Ocean, from which the ancestors of all American shamans arrived in the dim past. The sea-wolf lives yet, in the submarine energies which surround Vancouver Island and concentrate themselves at various sacred sites. Other images portrayed among the many dozens of petroglyphs include humans engaged in arcane ceremonial activities, but there is a stronger emphasis on sea creatures, particularly bottom fish.

The great care with which all the figures are executed, however simplistically, and the ten millennia during which they have been consistently venerated, irrevocably consecrate the area now known as Petroglyph Provincial Park as a sacred site of special power. The very stones resonate with 10,000 years of rituals, prayers and incantations. It is said the images themselves will come to life and speak in the dreams of anyone coming to them on behalf of a vision-quest.

Mystical Significance

Proceeding from the parking lot, visitors should leave their feelings open to the singular resonance of this sacred precinct. Following the trail through the woods should be experienced in the imagination as a way back into the primeval past, when the first humans to arrive at Vancouver Island trod this same ground. The atmospheric path soon opens into Petroglyph Provincial Park, and the evocative images of a profound antiquity are at hand.

The most powerful among them is certainly the sea-wolf mentioned above. While it appears malevolent, the creature actually represents ambivalent forces, if only because, taken singly, both the wolf and killer whale are Native American symbols for teaching and remembering, respectively—certainly, very positive functions. The sea-wolf is possibly a version of these symbolic beasts to describe the loss of the early inhabitants, who arrived at Vancouver Island as bedraggled survivors of the natural catastrophe that claimed the existence of their Pacific island home. The creature also appears to represent the energy which called the petroglyph center into being, since all sacred sites are material manifestations of the *genius loci*, or spirit of place that determines the sacred character of a particular location.

Petroglyph Park.   *Photo by Frank Joseph.*

But intellectually wrestling with precise meanings of the images will diffuse the higher, more precious experience of Petroglyph Provincial

Park. Allowing the rational mind to dominate one's visit diminishes the real value of an encounter by pushing the soul, or inner perceptions aside. It is primarily with our hearts, rather than our heads, that we should approach any sacred site. The petroglyphs are but physical keys to unlock far greater treasures than mere intellectual curiosity. Seeing the images in this light will lead to the psychic development they signify and trigger in our subconscious, a process wonderfully empowered by the resident energies of this potent sacred site.

Directions

Petroglyph Park lies off the main highway on the R, two-and-a-half miles (4 km) south of Nanaimo, which is sixteen miles (26 km) north of Ladysmith on Highway 1.

Information

Nanaimo Travel Info Center, 266 Bryden St., Nanaimo, B.C. V9S 1A8; tel. 1-800-663-7337; fax (250) 754-6468.

Source Notes

Dane, Christopher. *The American Indian and the Occult*, New York: Popular Library, 1973.

The Mysterious Mountain
Frank Joseph

In the summer of 1882, miners were working along the Dease Creek, which flows down from the Cassiar Mountain Range in the northwestern territory of British Columbia. Some twenty-four feet (8 m) below the mineral-rich sand, they were surprised to find thirty very curious-looking coins strung together, but they fell apart when one of the men tried to pick them up.

Two years after their discovery, they came into the possession of James Deans, a writer for a prominent scientific journal of the time, *American Naturalist*. Suspecting their Asian origins, he took the coins to an Oriental scholar (Chu Chong) in Victoria, who positively dated them to a Chinese Emperor, Huungti, who, the magazine reported, ruled in 2637

B.C. This date is problematical, because the Chinese did not use coined money until many centuries later. David Hatcher Childress, President of the World Explorers Club, writes "that the date is obviously a typographical error. The story is referring to Emperor Chi-Hunang-ti, the same emperor who built the Great Wall, had every book in China destroyed by royal command, and left an army of full-sized clay warriors in a pyramid near Xian, China.

"The period of his life was the Ch'in dynasty, which is typically dated as from 221 to 207 B.C. Therefore, the date of 263 B.C. for the 'chronological cycle of sixty years' would be more correct. Emperor Chi-Huang-ti is also known to have sent a huge expedition of thousands of men and women in an armada of huge junks to the 'Golden Land' in search of the 'magic fungus of immortality.' The expedition failed to return, and lacking the 'magic fungus,' the emperor died circa 207 B.C. One wonders if this expedition ended up in British Columbia."

But the Dease Creek discovery was not the first of its kind. In 1801, when British Columbia was still a colony, a single copper coin was found in a natural fresh-water spring not far from the Chilcotin River and taken to the nearby town of Chillicothe. Ink impressions of the raised characters on both sides of the artifact were made by John S. Willis and sent to the curator of the Philadelphia Museum (Pittsburgh, U.S.A.). Resident numismatists compared the Canadian impressions with "four pieces of copper coin procured at different times from China, which are exactly similar to the one found in the spring at Chillicothe." Will presented the coin to the governor of St. Clair.

That both discoveries, separated by more than eighty years, were made at important river systems tend to validate the authenticity of the coins. Ancient Chinese travelers penetrating the British Columbian interior from the coast would have taken advantage of these natural waterways. The coins are not the only evidence of an ancient Asian impact in the same area. Childress explains, "In the 1920s, the distinguished folklorist Marius Barbeau first noted the melodic resemblance between traditional funerary songs sung by Buddhists in Asia and those sung by Indians on the reserves along the banks of the Nass and Skeena Rivers in northern British Columbia. Barbeau noted that the tune scaled a high curve, touched a top note, then dropped over wide intervals to the bottom, where it droned leisurely. He reasoned that the songs came from 'a common Asiatic source.'"

Chinese visitors did indeed appear to have sailed to the northwestern territories of British Columbia in ancient times. But why they would have risked such a voyage (voyages?) was not made clear until a mineralogist, James Brett, made his own discovery in 1986. He knew that the Chinese of the midthird millennium B.C. regarded jade as necessary for the soul to achieve immortality after physical death. In dynastic funeral practices, shaped pieces of jade were placed over the eyes, nostrils, ears and mouth of the deceased. Emperors were put to rest in coffins carved entirely from jade. The ancient Chinese believed jade assisted mothers giving birth, cured disease, brought good luck and granted long life to anyone who possessed it. A jade cup from the second century B.C. bears the inscription, "May the sovereign of men have his longevity prolonged." The mineral was also used on a large scale in making jars, cups, rings, amulets, ritual discs, carvings, mirrors, musical instruments, statuary and numerous varieties of ceremonial objects, all esteemed the most valuable articles belonging to Chinese religious culture. According to Gunnar Thompson, jade was valued more highly than gold. As the respected mythographer, Donald A. Mackenzie, wrote, "One's thoughts at once turn to China when mention is made of jade, for in no other country in the world has it been utilized for such a variety of purposes or connected more closely with the social organization and with religious beliefs and ceremonies."

Interestingly, sources for green jade do not exist in China. Actual jadeite was not used by the Chinese until only 300 years ago, when it was imported for the first time from Burma. Until then, white jade (nephrite)

The Mysterious Mountain or Dark Mountain in the Cassiar Range.　*Photo by Dennis Graf.*

was mostly obtained, sparingly, from Lake Baikal (in eastern Siberia), Yarkand (an oasis in the far north, its people defiant of Chinese attempts at conquest until the mideighteenth century A.D.) and Kashgar (another distant oasis beyond Chinese grasp until 1755). These and all other sources of nephrite, known to the Chinese as *yu*, were regarded as barbarian countries by Chinese priests, who were willing to travel great distances for the mineral of immortality.

A Chinese document with origins in 250 B.C. tells of an important but far-distant location for nephrite. In Book VIII of the Shan Hai Jing, the anonymous author describes "White Jade Mountain," a sacred peak set aside by the gods in a cold and forested land far across the Eastern Sea. White Jade Mountain appears marked on the so-called "Harris Map," an English cartographer's rendering of traditional Chinese folklore. Several lines of the map leading toward the sacred mountain resemble the Fraser River, in British Columbia. Curiously, several spaces around White Jade Mountain are labeled "Entrails Country" and "No Entrails Country," which may have referred to good and bad hunting areas, respectively. If so, then this far-off source for nephrite was visited at least from time to time by Chinese miners, who stayed long enough to excavate sufficient quantities of the mineral. That the ancient Chinese possessed the maritime technology needed to bring them to British Columbia has been abundantly demonstrated by researcher Gunnar Thompson in two books, *American Discovery* and *Nu Sun: Asian-American Voyages*, 500 B.C.

When Brett learned of the Chinese coins in Canada, he found their original locations on modern maps of the Yukon headwaters. As he examined his sources, he was amazed to learn that the area of the Cassiar Mountain Range, where the 1881 discovery of the coins was made, is the largest source for jade in North America and one of the best in the world. As the renowned researcher, Donald L. Cyr, has written, "And thus, the importance of jade, the location of Chinese coins at Cassiar, the possibility of water travel up the Yukon from China, and the account of the Shan Hai Jing that seems to rename locations and mountains in North America seem to fit together."

Mystical Significance

The Chinese miners who voyaged across the broad and hazardous expanses of the Pacific Ocean to British Columbia were not engaged in an ordinary economic enterprise. They were on a quest for *yu*, the Night

Shining Jewel of immortality. The earliest coin found during 1801 in a fresh-water spring implies that it had been placed there deliberately as an offering to the spirit of White Jade Mountain. Such votive gestures were common throughout China all the way up to the Communist Revolution of 1949.

The spiritual energies early Chinese pilgrims brought to the holy mountain rendered it a sacred site and consecrated the mineral itself. Although less able than quartz crystal to facilitate the psychic vibrations set in motion by a person in an altered state of consciousness, jade, especially nephrite, is reputed to help achieve a level of serenity necessary for deep meditation. Its hazy matrix is at least symbolic of the "clouds of bliss" a spiritual adept attains on his way to inner enlightenment. White Jade Mountain was a place that drew psychic practitioners from the other side of the world.

But with the decline of their dynastic civilization, and especially as jade became available from barbarian countries closer to home, long voyages across the Sea of the Sunrise were no longer necessary. White Jade Mountain was no longer visited and all knowledge of the sacred site went to sleep in the realm of myth. The discovery of ancient Chinese coins at North America's foremost source of white jade, however, summons the legendary mount back to life in our own time.

The exact location of White Jade Mountain is not known. That it lies among the Cassiar Range is certain. Those summits closest to Dease Creek, where the coins were found in 1882, are its most obvious candidates. If expeditions were mounted to investigate their peaks for evidence of ancient mining, the location of White Jade Mountain might be established. Persons searching for it today resume the quest undertaken more than three millennia ago. Meanwhile, it must remain Canada's elusive, mysterious mountain.

Directions

A good candidate for the Cassiar's sacred site is Dark Mountain, located twenty-five miles (40 km) due east of Dease Lake, fifty miles (80 km) southeast from the town of Cassiar, which is reached via Highway 37 north from Terrace and other points south. Dease Lake is located forty miles (65 km) north of Iskut on Highway 37.

Source Notes

Berton, Pierre. *The Mysterious North*, Toronto: McClelland & Stewart, 1956.

Columbo, John Robert. *Mysterious Canada*, Toronto: Doubleday of Canada, 1990.

The Beast of Okanagan Lake
Frank Joseph

The large town of Kelowna is known to some as "British Columbia's answer to the French Riviera" for its attractive lake-front atmosphere. Each summer, tourists from all over Canada are drawn to its numerous daytime recreational activities and vibrant nightlife. Most of them have at least heard of another attraction not subject to the local travel bureau. For in the waters of Lake Okanagan fronting Kelowna a great and mysteriously elusive creature is supposed to make its home.

Dubbed Ogopogo after a popular English music hall song of 1924, the beast was known for countless centuries before to various Interior Salish tribes who resided at its lakeshore. They knew it as N'ha'-a-itk, or Something Powerful. The Chinook referred to it as the Wicked One and the Great Beast in the Lake. To countless generations of these Native Americans, the phenomenon was no laughing matter. In fact, the antiquity of human culture around Lake Okanagan is great. A fragment of worked elk antler found near the south shore was carbon-dated to 2,300 years ago. Perhaps even from that remote period, the indigenous people knew there was something monstrous about the lake.

The various historic Indian tribes regarded it as an entirely real creature, and always carried dogs or chickens aboard their canoes to throw overboard as a precautionary measure and alternative meals for N'ha-a-itk. An area 127 square miles (329 sq. km), Lake Okanagan would appear large and old enough to contain some mystery. It was formed 10,000 years ago by the last glacier that retreated north at the end of the Ice Age, leaving a body of water sixty-nine miles long but less than three miles at its widest point. White people began settling around its shores in the midnineteenth century, just when the earliest documented sightings of the creature are recorded. In July, 1890, a renowned sea captain, Thomas Shorts, was commanding the steamer *Jubilee* off Squally Point, where N'ha-a-itk was said to dwell in a submarine cave near Rattlesnake Island, south of Kelowna. Captain Shorts testified that he saw a fifteen-foot-long serpent on the surface with a head similar to that of a ram and broad fins thin enough through which he could see the sun shine.

Sightings of the beast increased along with the lake-shore population, so much so several cities and towns organized hunting parties determined to snare the creature. Personal observations were certainly in the hundreds before the Second World War and no doubt multiplied many times since. The beast has been the subject of numerous radio and television documentaries and newspaper articles. The leading expert on the Okanagan phenomenon is Arlene B. Gaal, whose books *Beneath the Depths* and *Ogopogo: The Million Dollar Monster* represent authoritative, convincing research. She says there are an average of seven to ten reported sightings of the creature each year. "In other years," Gaal says, "you're looking at as many as fifteen people at once spotting Ogo from a bus. In 1969, there were twenty-nine reported sightings."

A typical documented observation was made by Kelowna resident, Lillian Vogelgesang: "My daughter came running up from the beach white-faced shouting, 'It's a whale!' She was just ten, so I told her no, it must be a boat. Then I looked and it was right off the dock, three main humps undulating and splashing up waves. It was dark, dark slimy green. You could hear me scream three miles away. There was another lady there, and we both agreed it looked faster than a motorboat. My attitude used to be, I'll believe it when I see it. Now I don't care who believes it. That was years ago, and I can still see that green slime. My daughter won't go in the lake to this very day."

N'ha-a-itk's official recognition has certainly come of age. The Kelowna Chamber of Commerce pledged to finance the captured creature's transportation to Scotland, where mating with its European counterpart in Loch Ness was envisioned. The Kelowna City Hall is adorned with a metropolitan emblem featuring the image of a grizzly bear at the left and, on the right, the figure of Ogopogo. The former signifies Okanagan, the

Salish word for the animal. In the 1980s, Lloyd's of London had a standing offer of one million dollars to anyone who captured the beast. The British Columbia Department of Recreation and Conservation set up a plaque on Highway 97, describing N'ha-a-itk at the eastern shore between the towns of Peachland and Penticton. Beside Kelowna, there is another large effigy representing the monster on the north end of the lake, at the city of Vernon. The reinforced concrete statue rears its head from a duck pond in Polsen Park and shoots a stream of water from its gaping jaws.

John Fisher, a spokesman for the Canadian Tourist Association, promised $5,000 for a credible photograph of the real lake monster. No one has been able to collect the cash reward, despite some intriguing film footage. In 1963, the American Society of Ichthyologists met in a five-day conference at Kelowna to ostensibly study the possibility of a large, unknown creature in Lake Okanagan. Having made up their minds long

A re-creation of Ogopogo pulled through the waters of Lake Okanagan.
Photo by Klaus Goedecke of Kelowna. Reproduced with permission.

before their tongue-in-cheek get-together, the salaried experts predictably dismissed the whole phenomenon as a combined hoax and the misperceived sightings of unprofessional observers, who were obviously mistaking a line of beavers for some fabulous monster. They went on to argue that a fifty- to seventy-foot-long (17 to 25 m) creature would be unable to fit into the food-chain of the lake. How could the beast reproduce itself with such a conjecturedly small population over the course of centuries? And why have no carcasses of the animal ever been found, they wondered?

Despite these scientific misgivings, visitors and townsfolk alike continue to glimpse from time to time a huge, living creature slithering across the waters of Okanagan Lake.

Mystical Significance

The mystery of Ogopogo is an enduring enigma without physical evidence. Perhaps thousands of persons, the vast majority of them sober, qualified witnesses, have all seen the same creature in Lake Okanagan since its first documented observation in 1860. Unrecorded encounters experienced by generations of Indian tribes which passed through the area push the phenomenon into prehistory. There can be no doubt that something more extraordinary than a line of swimming beavers inhabits the waters.

Why, then, have no remains of a dead N'ha-a-itk washed ashore in all the years (centuries, millennia?) it supposedly inhabited the lake? For all the thousands of tourists armed with first home movie cameras and now, in far greater profusion, cam-corders, not a single, unequivocal photographic image of the creature has so far been taken. Ogopogo presents a contradiction of the first order: an over-abundance of eyewitnesses opposed by a total absence of material proof. What can we possibly conclude from such a disparity of evidence?

Perhaps the beast seen by so many persons does not belong to a material level of existence, but sometimes crosses over into our realm of the senses from its true habitat in another dimension. The facts that are available suggest as much. In Mrs. Vogelgesang's rather typical sightings mentioned above, she went on to say, "But later the other lady said she didn't see it." Here the Lake Okanagan problem shares a theme common to other phenomena reported by numerous, competent eye-witnesses, but lacking physical proof; namely, Sasquatch and UFOs. In many such sightings, one witness will have a clear view of the event, while a person standing beside him will see nothing.

We would do well to know that Lake Okanagan was revered as a sacred site by Native peoples almost certainly for thousands of years. Not far is the Keremeos Mound, described earlier. The Indians who venerated the lake were tribes of the Interior Salish Indians, as distinguished from the Salish who lived near the Pacific coast. At the center of their belief system was the concept of the Spirit Guardian. It was not one deity but many and took the form of a powerful animal, most often a monstrous serpent. Its chief duties were to protect sacred sites and to escort the souls of deceased persons from this life to the next. All the Indian tribal peoples of British Columbia still hold fast to their worship of Spirit Guardians. That two persons standing in close proximity to N'ha-a-itk should have vastly different interpretations of the encounter suggests that one of the observers, for whatever causes, was receptive to the energy surges peculiar to Lake Okanagan, while his or her companion was not.

In most, if not all sacred sites, visitors often experience an indefinable but palpable presence. The sensation appears to be related to the human brain's primeval reaction to the telluric forces operating at a place of earth-power. Such undulating energies sometimes appear in our perceptions as a living creature progressing in serpentine movement. Ogopogo is not unlike the dragon of Ancient and Medieval Europe, as well as Ancient Asia. Then as now, human beings were reacting on some fundamental level to the fluctuating power of the Earth at a holy spot.

N'ha-a-itk is not a fugitive from the age of dinosaurs. Real as he is, his carcass will never be found, and trying to capture him on film is like trying to photograph a dream. Because he comes from the same place; namely, the subconscious mind stimulated by particular energies of the sacred site at Lake Okanagan.

Directions

N'ha-a-itk has been observed at various locations across Okanagan Lake, although its lair and many sightings occur off Squally Point on Rattlesnake Island, just south of Kelowna. Other successful vantage-points may be found at the lakefront City Park, Strathcona Park, Boyce Gyro Park or Mission Beach Park. Kelowna is thirty-seven miles (60 km) north of Penticton, on Highway 97.

Information

Kelowna Travel Info Center, 544 Harvey Avenue, Kelowna, B.C., V1Y 6C9; tel. (250) 861-1515, or 1-800-663-4345; fax (250) 861-3624.

Source Notes

Gaal, Arlene B. *Beneath the Depths*, Okanagan Valley: Valley Review Publishing, Ltd., 1976.

Meurger, Michel and Claude Gagnon, *Lake Monster Traditions*, London: Fortean Times, 1988.

In Search of Dimlahamid
Frank Joseph

The numerous Indian tribes of Canada are as different from each other in language, customs and material culture as are the various nationalities of Europe. Yet, for all their tribal diversity, a single mythic theme binds them together, and it is still sung in ancestral chants and may even be traced in some of their traditional handiwork.

The We'suwet'en and Gitksan tribes of northern British Columbia probably preserve the most detailed account of a former time and place, from which all tribes originally descended. They tell of a huge civilization spread out for many miles along the Bulkley and Skeena Rivers. It was here that the great city of Dimlahamid towered toward the heavens. Other tribes remember the metropolis as Dzilke, but the essential account or myth allows little variation from group to group. To say that it has been known across the length and breadth of Canada from a deeply prehistoric period is no overstatement. The story is preserved in the Saga of Medeek, a powerful spirit, half-bear, half-lion, who seems to have personified the destructive forces of the universe.

Dimlahamid or Dzilke was mighty and supreme over much of the world for many years. In time, however, internal wars led to increasing strife, which offended the gods of nature. They punished Dimlahamid with a series of unprecedented earthquakes that shook the fabulous city and its sinful residents to destruction. Up-rooted trees were propelled through the air, mountains crumbled, rivers, lakes and the seas swelled suddenly, spilling floods over the trembling land. In the midst of this horrible chaos, Medeek himself appeared. He joined the destruction, annihilating everything and anyone in his way. Even the splendid Street of the Chiefs collapsed into ruin. The capital was finally overwhelmed by a watery cataclysm and buried by the Earth itself. The few survivors went their own ways to eventually sire the various Native tribes of Canada.

Critics of the myth point out that it is specifically used by the Wet'suwet'en and Gitksan, its greatest narrators, in their legal struggles for land rights throughout the Queen's courts of British Columbia. By establishing their great Native antiquity, they hope to justify their claims. But knowledge of Dzilke was already wide-spread when the first European settlers arrived in Canada. Remarkably, the myth contains very few religious elements, because the Native peoples regarded Dimlahamid as a real place, and not as a spiritual conception of the celestial city.

The first scientific search for Dzilke was undertaken by professional anthropologist, Edward Sapir, in 1915. Although unable to find any physical evidence, Sapir did determine that all the Pacific coast clans gathered at a central place known as Dimlahamid, from which they established themselves over hundreds of thousands of square miles of territory. In 1923, decades before Indian land disputes began, the vast extent of the Dzilke myth was gauged by an enthusiastic amateur, Constance Cox, who personally sought out the story from Kam Ya'en, chief of the Firewood tribe, in Gitsegukla. Her work was confirmed and expanded upon by the renowned Canadian anthropologists, Marius Barbeau and Diamond Jenness.

The first really serious expedition to find remains of Dimlahamid got under way in 1966, when the National Museum of Man dispatched survey crews and field-veteran archaeologists into the area between the Bulkley and Skeena Rivers. Not a trace of the lost city was found. The search was resumed by various researchers, mostly non-Indian, throughout the 1970s. They concentrated their efforts among the hills and valleys from Moricetown to Gitsegukla, without success. Despite many and failed attempts to recover a shred of physical proof, the Native tribal peoples of Canada in general and British Columbia particularly are convinced that Dimlahamid was a real place, the vanished homeland of their ancestors.

Mystical Significance

Investigators of Dimlahamid are perplexed, because it is part of an historical myth. It is not a mere fable or moral tale. Myth is the means by which a non-literate people preserve their folk memory. Dimlahamid did indeed exist, as Edward Sapir concluded. He said it represented a center or midpoint for prehistoric clans. The very name is not at home in any Indian language; nor is "Dzilke." Where did theses names come from? And why has not a stick of the lost city been found, if it did exist, as the Indians insist? It is remarkable that the various tribes would have even conceived of a metropolis for their origins, because they never built

In search of Dimlahamid.   *Artwork by Kenneth Caroli.*

anything even remotely resembling a city, let alone the megalopolis Dzilke was supposed to have been. In truth, the myth has every appearance of an import, of having been brought to the Indians from outside.

The story of Dimlahamid somewhat resembles the story of Atlantis, a resemblance made closer by comparing the dates for either catastrophe. According to Terry Glavin, a reporter for the *Vancouver Sun* newspaper, in his book, *A Death Feast at Dimlahamid*, the Saga of Medeek dates Dzilke's last day to 3,500 years ago. The proper lunar date for the final destruction of Atlantis is around 1200 B.C. The three-century difference is relatively insignificant when attempting to place historic events within useful time parameters through the agency of comparative myth. Other investigators conclude Dimlahamid was not Atlantis but another famous lost civilization that perished even earlier, the sunken island of Mu, in the Pacific Ocean. Either of these interpretations is attractive, because the apparent lack of any archaeological evidence contrasts too sharply with the universal permanence and uniformity of Native tradition.

That Dimlahamid was a real place seems clear, especially to the masses of Indian peoples in British Columbia. Perhaps, in view of the millennia which separate them from the event, they transposed the Atlantis or Mu in myth from their oceanic realms to the territory between the Bulkley and Skeena Rivers, which symbolically represented the sea surrounding the ancestral homeland. This explanation alone seems to satisfy both the utter dearth of material finds and the endurance of an historic tribal memory. If so, then the lands embraced by these two rivers comprise a true sacred site. Visitors there will find no ruined towers of a once-glorious civilization, because all its splendid walls and glittering palaces lie, not below British Columbian soil, but under some distant sea. Here, however, the memory of that magical, vanished capital lives in the thoughts of its ultimate descendants. Search as we may for Dzilke's Street of the Chiefs despoiled by Medeek, we shall not find it, save in the magical milieu, created through the power of undying belief, of the hills and valleys between the Bulkley and Skeena Rivers. As such, Dimlahamid exists yet in the folkish memory of too many Native peoples for dismissal as pure fantasy.

Directions

What might be termed Dzilke-energies may be experienced at various locations between the Bulkley and Skeena Rivers. There are a number of sites in the area still venerated by Native peoples for the strong feeling of Dimlahamid sensed there, but they are remote, sometimes hidden and probably guarded and, therefore, "off-limits" to most outsiders.

A location most definitely open and a good beginning to any search for Dimlahamid is the village of Telkwa, in the Bulkley Mountains. Its name is certainly suggestive of the elusive sacred center; in Wet'sewet'en, it means, "where the waters meet." Nearby is the Driftwood Canyon Provincial Park, another intriguing candidate for the lost civilization. It is the former bottom of a lake that disappeared through a series of massive volcanic eruptions and chasm-splitting earthquakes. Fossils of fish, beetles and other insects, together with the leaves of dawn redwood, oak, pine cypress, birch, horsetails and ferns are embedded in shale formed when masses of fine, volcanic ash settled on the dying lake.

A living lake, Tyhee, only two-minutes' drive from Telkwa, is another location associated with Dzilke energies. Telkwa lies six miles (10 km) east of Smithers on Highway 16.

Information

Village of Telkwa, Box 220 (NW), Telkwa, B.C. V0J 2X0; tel. (250) 846-5212; fax 846-9572.

Source Notes

Childress, David Hatcher. *Lost Cities of North & Central America*, Stelle, Illinois: Adventures Unlimited Press, 1992, pp. 257–259.

Glavin, Terry. *A Death Feast in Dimlahamid*, Vancouver: New Star Books, 1990.

Sasquatch
Frank Joseph

In early summer, a pair of prospectors in southwest British Columbia were intrigued to find a line of tracks belonging to some animal beyond their imagining. The men saw that the imprints were fresh, so, shouldering their hunting rifles, they decided to follow the man-like footprints through the lonely mountains northwest of Pitt Lake. The tracks had been made by a creature with feet twice as long as their own, and were particularly unusual, in that they were perfectly flat and showed only four toes. Judging from the length between prints, the prospectors judged the beast which made them walked up-right like a man, but at double the stride.

Neither man knew what to expect, as they followed the strangely pink-tinted tracks to the other side of Lake Pitt close to noon. There, they came to some trees, and half-hidden among the branches was a hulking animal standing ten feet (3 m) tall. It neither ran nor attacked at the prospectors' careful approach, but eyed them alertly, as it gently swayed back and forth, as though rhythmically shifting its weight, its pendulous

B.C.: Kispiox. A Gitksan Indian offertory vessel or ritual object of the type used by shamans to connect with non-material Otherworld behind the Natural World. The red bands and neck signify blood or the physical component of our human existence, while brown represents Earth. In between these bands, white stands for the spiritual dimension underlying and ordering nature.

Photo by James Lee.

B.C.: "In Search of Dimlahamid." *Original artwork by Max Lopez.*

Utah: Zion National Park. A fossilized giant from the Age of Mammals.
Photo courtesy Zion National Park.

Yukon and Northwest Territories: Nahanni. Overlooking Nahanni National Park.

Photo by Dennis Graf.

B.C.: Nimpkish. The frame of a sacred "long house" under construction, using traditional methods. *Photo by Carol Rumann.*

B.C.: Writing-on-Stone.

B.C.: The Cadborosaurus of Victoria. "Water Monster."

Artwork by Mary Robertson.

B.C.: Where Eagles Gather. "The Spirit of Squamish Eagledom," original sculpture at the Squamish Library.

Photo by Frank Joseph.

B.C.: The Columneetza Stone.

Photo by Frank Joseph.

Oregon: Wizard Island.

Photo by Richard Ely.

Saskatchewan: Medicine Wheels.

B.C.: Chemainus. "Native Heritage."

Right: **B.C.: Chemainus.** "1891."
Photo by Lorne Green. Courtesy of Chemainus Mural Society, all rights reserved.

Left: **B.C.: Chemainus.**
Photo by Lorne Green. Courtesy of Chemainus Mural Society, all rights reserved.

Below: **B.C.: Chemainus.** "First Sight."
Photo by Lorne Green. Courtesy of Chemainus Mural Society, all rights reserved.

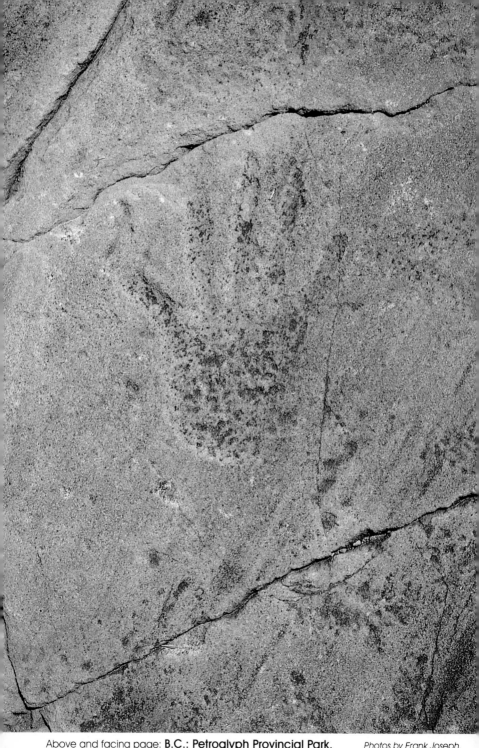

Above and facing page: **B.C.: Petroglyph Provincial Park.** *Photos by Frank Joseph.*

Alaska: Mount McKinley. *Photo courtesy of Alaska Department of Tourism.*

Montana. *Photo courtesy of Travel Montana Department of Commerce, Helena, MT.*

B.C.: Thunderbird Park.

Photo by Dennis Graf.

Utah: Zion National Park. Apollo's Blessing.   *Photo by Frank Joseph.*

B.C.: "The Search for Dimlahamid." *Artwork by Kenneth Caroli.*

Above and Left: **Alberta: Writing-on-Stone.** The Badlands.

Photos by Dennis Graf.

Right: **Alberta: Writing-on-Stone.** The Badlands.

Artwork by Kenneth Caroli.

arms hanging loose and exceedingly muscular. The beast was entirely covered with long, auburn hair, save for its massive hands, which verged on yellow, and its face, which was bare and flat-featured, essentially simian in appearance, but not without some human quality around the eyes. Although upright, the creature stooped its bulky shoulders. It continued to sway on its heels and stare fixedly at the two men, who beat a slow retreat. They cautiously returned later in the afternoon to the place of encounter. Only fresh tracks among the trees remained to mark the spot where the animal had stood.

That meeting between man and man-beast in 1965 was typical of the hundreds of modern reports, before and since, which form some of the documentation for the existence of Sasquatch. The animal is generally described as anthropomorphic, with somewhat human facial features, eight to twelve feet (3 to 4 m) in height, between 800 and 1,000 pounds (360 and 450 kg), excessively hairy, omnivorous, mostly but not exclusively nocturnal, often sighted near water, evil-smelling but essentially gentle and solitary. Arguments on behalf of Sasquatch are usually divided into four categories: Native American tradition, modern eyewitnesses, footprints and photographic documents. Native legends are among the most significant evidence because of their antiquity and their close parallel with present-day experiences. The very name is persuasive that the phenomenon is authentic, because it derives from Indian accounts which go back into prehistory, and are, therefore, not limited to present-day sightings only. No hoax could endure countless generations of observations identically described by eyewitnesses from two radically different cultures.

Sasquatch is an Anglicization of the Chehalis word for the creature. The phenomenon is by no means confined to the Chehalis Indian Reserve near the Harrison River, but is known elsewhere in British Columbia as the *Boqs* to the Bella Coola Indians residing in the coastal region of Burke Channel, *Almasti* in Siberia, the *Yeti* in Nepal, the Abominable Snowman in the Himalayas and Bigfoot in Washington State, Oregon and northern California. This broadly international scope of sightings argues strongly in favor of their credibility.

Credible, too, are the many curious, so-called monkey masks carved usually from red cedar by various Indian craftsmen of the Pacific Northwest. Examples are on display at Toronto's Royal Ontario Museum, Harvard University's Peabody Museum and Victoria's Royal British Columbia Provincial Museum. They are outstanding examples from the

Tsimshian and Niska tribes of the northern province, along the Nass River. It goes without saying that the nearest monkeys can be found many thousands of miles away in the jungles of Central America, and that the Indians of upper British Columbia had no personal experience of these primates. The carvings far more likely represent Sasquatch, with which the Indians were and are long familiar, at least in myth. And the fact that these objects were used as ceremonial masks further identifies them with the legendary spirit of the forest.

Mystical Significance

Sasquatch, lake monsters, UFOs and ghosts are phenomena which share a common theme: they are witnessed by numerous, credible observers but leave no physical proof of their existence. There are more than 3,000 documented sightings of Sasquatch and his counterparts in other parts of the world. Many of these reports were made by persons of impeccable personal credentials. Yet, the only material finds for the creature are approximately 700 descriptions of circa seventeen-inch (27 cm) footprints, some preserved in plaster or latex molds. But even this body of evidence is equivocal. Those examples which appear genuine are still problematical, because impressions made in snow or even mud tend to substantially elongate and even distort by the force exerted to make them. Even so, the noted taxidermist, Robert Titmus, of Kitimat, British Columbia, was convinced that tracks he saw in northern California belonged to a Sasquatch.

There are no photographs of such a creature and only a single, overexposed, twenty-four-foot strip of 16-mm movie film believed by some

Bigfoot investigator Cliff Crook with cast of footprint in Washington where a creature was reported.　　　　*Photograph © by Cliff Crook.*

to show Bigfoot striding through the thickly wooded Bluff Creek area of northern California. Scientific opinion about the Patterson Film was divided after it was first shown in 1967. Dr. Grover Krantz at the University of Minnesota concluded, "I am absolutely satisfied that the movie subject is a living, breathing Sasquatch, not 98 percent or 99 percent but 100 percent certain it is real." Dr. Bernard Joseph Heuvelmans did not agree. "The motion picture taken in California of what is obviously a man dressed in a monkey-suit made of nylon fur," was the judgement of the famous Belgian zoologist. He was seconded by scholars Ciochon, Olsen and James, who were just as unconvinced by the footage: "A further objection is the creature's gait, which is suspiciously human-looking." Responded Canadian researcher, Rene Dahinden, "You cannot put a fur suit on somebody and then see all the muscle masses moving, because a fur suit really conceals all this. It doesn't walk like a human being." Dahinden showed the Patterson film to a professional body-builder. "His comment was that all the muscle masses are all in the proper places and if you have heavy muscles on the buttocks, you have to have attachments for all these muscles." Danny Perez, who heads the Center for BigFoot Studies, says, "If the film is in fact a fake, a costumed man or a machine, surely science could duplicate the film with ease. Twenty-five years later, no one has come close."

The critics also point to the total absence of a Sasquatch carcass. For all the decades or centuries of reports, the dead body of a single BigFoot has never been recovered. Is it conceivable, they ask, that a family or families of large creatures could have consistently escaped detection or capture for so long? Certainly an honest researcher of the phenomenon, John Green, of Agassiz, British Columbia, writes, "Whether a real creature is responsible for the many eyewitness reports of giant, hairy bipeds in North America has not been established, and that may remain the case for many years." Perez believes "that some thing is behind the literature, ghost or physical animal, uncaught, unclassified and unbottled by twentieth-century science."

If Sasquatch is not "a physical animal," it might be a projection of the subconscious mind stimulated by the earth-energies (seismic action) common to places venerated for their spiritual power. In fact, there appears to be a recognizable correlation between sightings of the creature and sacred sites. In the U.S., Bigfoot encounters are reported in the vicinity of Mt. St. Helens, infamous for its geologic instability and long venerated by Native Americans for its *genius loci*. In British Columbia, eyewitness accounts occur between the Bulkley and Skeena Rivers, perhaps the most hallowed ground in Native America (see In Search of Dimlahamid). The creature has been seen at Chilliwack Lake, not far from a famous haunted house (see The Chilliwack Ghosts). Sightings have been made around the Harrison Hot Springs, a seismic zone and regarded by local Indians as holy.

The creature is real, perhaps not so much on our material level of existence, as in our subconscious reaction to and visualization of telluric energy concentrated at certain places of Earth power we call sacred sites. If so, then Sasquatch is indeed the Spirit of the Forest, as known to Native Americans.

Directions

Sasquatch sightings occur throughout the deeply forested regions of British Columbia. But the Chehalis Indians, from who the name derives, believe the beast is most likely to be seen along the Harrison River in the vicinity of Chilliwack, 25 miles (40 km) east of Abbotsford on Highway 1, or sixty-four miles (103 km) east of Vancouver. Take Exit 116 or 119.

Information

Cliff Crook, Chairman, *Bigfoot Central*, North America's Bigfoot Research Foundation, PO Box 147 Bothell, WA 98041; tel. (206) 402-0614. *Bigfoot Central* provides the most thoroughly researched information on the Sasquatch phenomenon.

Source Notes

Green, John Willison. *On the Track of Sasquatch*, Books 1 & 2, British Columbia: Hancock House Publishers Ltd., 1980.

Knerr, Michael E. *Sasquatch, Monster of the Northwest Woods*, New York: Belmont Tower Books, 1977.

Perez, Danny. *Bigfoot Times*, 29 October 1992, Norwalk, CA: California Center for Bigfoot Studies.

Where Eagles Gather
Frank Joseph

Brooding high and mighty over the town of Squamish on the river of the same name are the towering monolith of Stawamus Chief and the Little Smoke Bluffs. Sunrise brings morning in a silence peculiar to this part of the world. Hardly a breeze stirs and a strange quiet pervades the vicinity throughout the first part of the day. But just at noon, strong winds suddenly arise to blast the valley with air currents strong enough to scoot windsurfers at speeds in excess of thirty-five miles per hour. Throughout the afternoon, the terrific winds howl over the land. Then, at evening twilight, the declining sun takes all turbulence with it into the night.

This somewhat eerie, certainly awesome location, with its daily, violent alterations of morning silence and afternoon tumult, possesses some unknown, numinous quality that occasions one of the great events of the natural world. Each autumn, a few days after the fall equinox, an annual wind descends on the Squamish vicinity. It is caused by the thunderous beating of innumerable pairs of gigantic, powerful wings. They beat together in such dense numbers, they collectively form an impossibly huge, black sky-beast with thousands of eyes, talons and beaks, roaring on the gusts of afternoon turbulence like a terrible, thousand-throated god. This is the yearly arrival of eagles, possibly the greatest convocation of its kind on Earth.

In 1994, more than 3,700 of the enormous birds were counted in Squamish. Although their assembling is obviously part of an annual migration pattern, scientists do not understand why the eagles choose this location to gather in such impressive numbers. Food is actually more abundant in other locations at this time of year.

Whatever the cause or causes, the appearance of massed formations of eagles by the thousands descending on a location favored by instinct or some other power is the sight of a lifetime.

Mystical Significance

To the indigenous peoples of British Columbia, the eagle was sometimes regarded as a reincarnated shaman. The animal was believed to

117

personify the height of spiritual attainment and power. To even see an eagle was considered a blessing or an omen, because the bird was regarded as a connection to the Great Spirit. Its feathers were the most sacred healing tools, particularly for cleansing the human aura of all negativity.

The eagle signified, as it still does among many cultures, courage and triumph. Of course, any location where more than one would choose to flock was regarded as a sacred site for particular veneration. But Squamish, with its annual gathering of several thousand of the birds at one time, establishes a sacred center of the most extraordinary type. Local Indian tradition has long identified the area as a earth-power vortex or natural, unseen gateway between this world and the next. It is here that the spirit mystically assumes material form in the contrasting stillness and winds, but especially in the unheard call that summons the eagles all at once. The timing of their gathering is also significant, being as it is the moment that separates summer from autumn – from the fullness of life to its decline.

As mentioned earlier (In the Realm of Stillness), zones of profound silence are commonly associated with sacred sites everywhere. But the uncanny stillness at Squamish is unique, because it is the prelude to ferocious winds, upon whose backs clouds of eagles ride screaming each fall equinox. For the visitor to such a blessed place at such a dramatic time, the arrival of so many majestic birds can signify the triumph of Nature over mankind's ecological blasphemies.

More profoundly, we are made aware of some grand truth, its magnitude too great for expression in mere words. Like listening to and being deeply stirred by a piece of the most touching music, we cannot explain it; we may only feel it. But what feels at such a moment, if not our soul? This is the true experience and ultimate meaning of the sacred site, as exemplified once each year at Squamish.

Directions

Squamish is located thirty-seven miles (60 km) north of Vancouver on Highway 99.

Information

Squamish & Howe Sound Chamber of Commerce, 37950 Cleveland Ave., Squamish, B.C. V0N 3G0; tel. (604) 892-9344; fax (604) 892-2034.

Source Notes

Carson, David and Jamie Sams. *Medicine Cards, The Discovery of Power through the Ways of Animals*, Santa Fe, New Mexico: Bear & Company, 1988, pp. 41, 42.

Montana

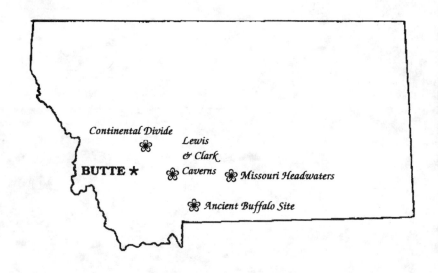

Continental Divide
❀

Lewis
& Clark
❀ *Caverns*   ❀ *Missouri Headwaters*

BUTTE ★

❀ *Ancient Buffalo Site*

Map Symbols

Natural Sacred Site --- ❀

Holy Mountain --- ▲

Sacred Space --- ●

Native American Site --- ❖

Medicine Wheel --- ✹

Ancient, Manmade Site --- ✠

Modern, Manmade Site --- ✿

Spectral Creature --- ?

Haunting --- ◇

Montana
Lynn Crowe and Sandra Rachlis

Land itself is holy in Montana, still the domain of massive beings living relatively undisturbed. In the east, rolling plains lead up to small mountain clusters—forerunners of the main body of the Rockies. Western Montana is filled with range after range of the Rocky Mountains. The truly awesome spaces of the state are alive with personalities and primal energy. In Montana, you can absorb holiness, and magically affirm your role in "all-that-is." It is an excellent place to speak prayers and intentions, to do "at-one-ment" rituals, and to perform ceremonies with the intent of increasing our planetary atunement with universal harmony.

Our approach is to help you participate with the abundant spirits of place in Montana. We'll teach you to find your own sacred places, and our perspective will assist in keying minds and hearts to Montana's powerful healing presences. Taught by the energies themselves, we're sharing a way of interacting with the sacredness of these lands.

Out of the Great Basin prairies, the high plains sweep toward the shining mountains. Surely these spaces are a living symbol of the ancient Medicine Wheel teachings. Here, you stand at the center of the horizon; 360 degrees of im-

Montana Glacier.
Photo Courtesy of Montana State Board of Tourism.

121

mense landscape meeting the sky. You are at the center, where Earth and sky meet is the perimeter of the wheel. This way of seeing the circle is always possible in a mountain valley or a forest grove. Magically recognizing and receiving the wheel is an excellent way to introduce yourself to spirits of place.

The four elements are dramatically alive in the land spaces of Montana. We have chosen to emphasize water, because the headwaters of the Missouri are here, a sacred center of a main life-giving aspect of our continent and the seas. Imbue the high mountain waters with your magical intentions and they will flow with the water throughout the continent and ultimately into the Ocean.

Montana is dry and even arid in parts, so water in these lands is sacred in several ways. Precipitation is light; what little rain and snow falls gives life to wild plants and animals, as well as to crops and herds. On a wider scale, the mountain near the Continental Divide stores snow that feeds the Columbia River and the Missouri-Mississippi drainage basin until the first rains of summer. The water table in the Rockies is the indicator of the health of continental water reserves. The lingering snows, and the mountains that conserve them, need our spiritual recognition as the lifegivers that they are.

The following is a detailed description of a segment of Montana that covers the stretch of country between Manhattan (Montana) and Butte. We're describing it east to west, but it works just fine from the opposite direction. For this entire area, stay on the frontage road, old US 10.

This is a pilgrimage between Manhattan and Butte, among the headwaters of the Missouri and some of the waters that feed it. At Three Forks, the Gallatin, Jefferson, and Madison Rivers come together to form the headwaters of the Missouri. Along this route, you can see a small herd of buffalo, Madison Buffalo Jump State Monument, the Missouri Headwaters State Park, Jefferson River Canyon, Lewis and Clark Caverns, the Continental Divide, Homestake Rock Shop at the top of the Divide, and at the western end, Butte—where you might pray for cleansing of the poisoned waters of the Earth and for the mountain which is there no more.

Start by getting off I-90 at Manhattan, and head west on the old highway. To the north and west are the Horseshoe Hills, where fossil hunters have found trilobite fossils and other remnants of ancient life forms. As you proceed toward Three Forks, watch to the left of the road for a small buffalo herd. This is a good opportunity to stop and make an offering to the buffalo, who once gave life to the humans of this part of

North America. At the village of Logan, five miles (9 km) west of Manhattan, turn off to the buffalo jump. Go south under the freeway and follow signs along the graded road.

Ancient Buffalo Site

Before the coming of the horse, indigenous North American hunters used natural cliff formations to kill a winter's meat supply by carefully guiding and stampeding the huge animals toward and over the brink. Other members of the group waited below to skin and butcher the harvest. This site is at least 500 years old, and was likely used much earlier.

The buffalo was holy to people of ancient times. The process of feeding and clothing the people, preparing meat and leather, was known to be a sacred work. Here is a good place to make an offering, and assure the buffalo of your respect for their lives and the on-going life force on the planet and continent. In this place, a good offering would be bits of fresh food left out in a sheltered spot for the spirits to share.

The Missouri

From Logan, travel five or six miles (10 km) to the turn for Missouri

Jefferson River, Montana.   *Photo courtesy Montana Department of Commerce.*

Headwaters State Park. This is where the three rivers merge. Here at the source of the Missouri, it is time to turn 360 degrees, recognize the six directions (the four cardinal directions as well as above and below), and invoke a blessing for this waterway and all the waters of the Earth. One water blessing that works for us, is to kneel at the edge of the wild water; scoop a handful of water and touch it to your forehead; take a second handful and touch it to your heart. Repeat the process. As you do this action, speak out loud, thanking the waters for their generosity and for the gift of life—yours, and on behalf of all beings. Be sure to include in your ceremony a mention of your intention that all of Earth's waters be beautiful and cleansed. Meditate for a while on the shore, feeling the birth of the great being that is the Missouri River.

At the headwaters you are touching United States heritage; here the explorers Lewis and Clark reached a part of their expeditionary goals. After you finish acknowledging the Power of the Waters, make a tobacco offering; verbally recognize how that expedition invited exploitation into these far mountains. The words should include a mention of how Earth-awareness has shifted among Lewis and Clark's people. Declare that you are working toward a balanced relationship among the sacred circle of life forms.

Butte

As you drop down from the Divide on the old highway into Butte, you will notice two things: the small city in the valley, and the mining scar to the north of the city. Butte, once known as the home of the Copper Kings, generated wealth for investors in the 1800s, when copper was discovered beneath the mountain where the original settlement stood. Millions were made from the "richest hill on earth"—a hill (actually a mountainside) which is no longer there, having been literally removed. The first mines were underground, honeycombed beneath the streets and homes of residents. Sometimes parts of Butte still cave in, when segments of the 10,000 miles of subterranean antic mining tunnels give way.

Even before you reach the city of Butte, driving in from any direction, you can note the nearby mountains that are bare of trees. These were cut down to provide structural timbers to shore up the early mine tunnels, and to be burned to provide energy for mining and smelting. It is ironic that the mountain named Timber Butte—now relatively barren—was one of the prime sources of such trees. So vast were the effects of the mining that even the weather changed. Because the trees were gone, the ground could no longer hold as much moisture from the yearly rains, and the region turned more arid. Because of the aridity, new seedling trees that might have replaced the cut ones have a poorer chance of survival.

Economic shifts during the 1960s led to pit mining for getting at the rich ores under the mountain. It didn't take long for open-pit mining to become the main process. By the late 1970s, most of the city on the mountain, and the mountain itself, were gone. Stores, homes, hotels and historic areas of the city were evacuated and swallowed by the expanding Berkeley Pit. The pit ate deeper and wider into the mountain, until it was a mile (1.6 km) deep and at least as wide. The city of Butte moved itself down into the valley, and continues to expand there. An auxiliary pit destroyed another landmark to the east of the original hole. The elegant Columbia Gardens, with its sculptured flower beds and lawns, antique carousel and roller coaster, was removed. The lovely Victorian amusement park disappeared along with the hillside it had formerly occupied.

Although the Berkeley Pit had been closed for several years, a new ecological threat has developed. The mile deep Berkeley Pit is filling rapidly with highly toxic water—at the rate of millions of gallons daily. This poisoned water is beginning to seep into the groundwater tables. Other old mining and abandoned industrial sites contribute additional noxious residues to surface waters with each spring's fresh runoff.

This situation is not being ignored. Butte and nearby Anaconda constitute the largest allocation of superfund monies set aside by the United States government to clean up the life-threatening aftermath of massive environmental destruction caused by industry.

Go to the Berkeley Pit viewing stand in the northeastern part of the city. In this location you have an opportunity for ceremonial healing—not only for the devastated mountainside in Butte, but for all the wounded landscapes planet-wide that have been brutalized by industrial society. The site of Butte, Montana, is not only a symbol for unmindful environmental exploitation, but also one of humans disregarding one another. The destruction of old Butte eliminated culturally rich Italian and Finnish neighborhoods. Regard Butte as a symbol of thoughtless development and charge the symbol with your healing intent. Butte is a place to effectively work for the health of the planet and for human awareness.

As you recognize and consider the wheel from Butte, your ceremonial purpose could be that what you observe here is the last of such a trend on our planet. Pray for reclamation of this and the many other such sites, and also for an awakening in the human spirit of a vision that will forever ensure a harmonious relationship between technological needs and the life force.

Our advice for approaching the above locations can serve as an example for anywhere you go.

Finding Your Own Sacred Places

There you are, driving along the freeway. You would like to have a little adventure, but don't know exactly where to go and how to get there.

If you have the time, it's a wonderful way to be able to get intimate with some area that strikes the right chord in your heart. Go on secondary roads so you can stop right away when you feel the impulse, or can turn around quickly instead of having to go thirty miles (49 km) before getting to the next freeway exit.

It is a physical fact that when you move slower, you see more, and thus you get a better sense of the neighborhood you're traveling through. You can also see in more detail the plants, trees, birds, animals, the little (and big) effects of water and its habits, and how the weather affects these living communities.

Stop and take out your map of Montana. Look for some indications from the symbols (see map legend) of national or state parks and campgrounds. These areas are designated because they are usually beautiful and powerful—so much so that someone thought it worthwhile to protect them from being logged or paved or subdivided. Sometimes these places are also just too wild to be accessible for economic development and they have kept their integrity, which you can feel as you travel near or through them. Usually, there are highway signs indicating turnoffs to national or state parks and public forest lands.

Once you're on a secondary road on the way to a chosen site, you may see brown forest service signs that indicate places of local interest. These are often worth investigating.For example: you're on a paved or graded road and there are many small dirt roads leading off it with brown signs that might have several places listed, such as Rainbow Lake—2 miles (3.5 km); Ranger Station—12 miles (20 km); or Perry's Meadows—3.5 miles

(6 km). Signs such as these are good indications that if you follow the road, you will find places of scenic beauty with public access.

So take the time to look, think about where you are, and consider how this spot relates to all within your field of vision. Frequently check on your inner awareness. Try to let yourself become merged with the sense of where you are. Stop the car if you need to and breathe, meditate or pray—whatever works for you. Get out of the car and listen for a while. If you find yourself moving into unusual levels of consciousness, follow yourself into them. You might find yourself going at a ridge, imagining you are a hawk flying along it; your body may feel an actual physical pull in that direction. Go toward the ridge. Or maybe you'll have a driving curiosity to know where that game trail goes that you notice on a hillside.

When these pulls or feelings happen, there is usually no distinction between person, thought and action. The next logical step, if the place is safe and you feel right, is to lace up your shoes and leave the car behind. Some people feel self-conscious out-of-doors, and have reservations about moving around freely. If you feel strongly drawn to some area, why shouldn't you go there if it's physically and legally feasible (that is, if it's not fenced private land)? You could walk up onto the mountain; a one-hour walk could lead you through juniper and cedar groves, pines and little gullies, delicate and fragile. You could be in an area frequented by owls, deer, eagles and bears.

Stay on paths or game trails, lest you damage friable soil structure. Off trail, there are spaces through which no one has walked for decades. The webs of strength and living interaction are palpable, and energy may be drawn from these spaces. Again, respect!

Source Notes

Henderson, Marlene. *My Montana*, Butte: Rustic Press Inc., 1949.

Montgomery, Ralph. *Montana—Flora, Fauna and Mountains*, New York: Doubleday Inc., 1983.

Swetzer, Judith. *Montana Guidebook Series*, Butte: State Press Inc., 1988.

Oregon

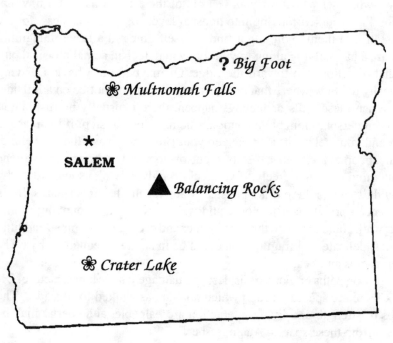

? Big Foot

❀ Multnomah Falls

★
SALEM

▲ Balancing Rocks

❀ Crater Lake

Map Symbols

Natural Sacred Site --- ❀

Holy Mountain --- ▲

Sacred Space --- ●

Native American Site --- ❖

Medicine Wheel --- ☸

Ancient, Manmade Site --- ⌗

Modern, Manmade Site --- ❦

Spectral Creature --- ?

Haunting --- ◇

Balancing Rocks
D. J. Conway

The Balancing Rocks, which are found in a little canyon in east-central Oregon, look like a scene from another world. They are on a barren, exposed hillside gulch formed by a prehistoric lava flow. The stark, hardpan slope is covered with conical stone spikes; each one, with a few exceptions, is topped with a flat stone large enough to overhang on the sides. Each balancing rock is unique. The canyon with its unusual formations looks like a forest of giant, weirdly-formed stone mushrooms. Visitors should be on the lookout for scorpions and rattlesnakes.

Around this little pink-toned valley is a backdrop of mountains and flat-topped mesas sprinkled with a few dark green pines. It is very unlikely that you will have to share the canyon with other tourists; as the Balancing Rocks are not publicized, nor are they well-known to most Oregonians. A

Oregon Balancing Rocks.   *Illustration by William Wild.*

129

cave in the immediate vicinity is said to contain Indian petroglyphs, but we were unable to locate it.

Mystical Significance

The Balancing Rocks were regarded as sacred by various local Indian tribes for generations stretching back into prehistory. The site was venerated as much for its profound silence, as for the dreamlike character of its colossal formations, the result of erosional forces at work for unknown millennia. While evidence of neither human burials nor ceremonial centers has been found in the area, the ongoing Native American tradition of ritual veneration defines Balancing Rocks as an enduring sacred site.

But visitors unaware of local (and undisclosed) Indian practices are by no means prevented from experiencing the singular awe generated by the environment. The strange and powerful contrast of profound silence in the presence of the gargantuan rock towers is among the moving characteristics of this unworldly place. We may feel somewhat overawed by confrontation with the Earth Mother in her weird attire, but her energies do not seem threatening, just monumental. Her grand, geologic chess pieces seem to imply the core principle of Nature itself—the subtle balance of forces. There too, is a lesson for us, in that we should strive for a balance of forces in our own lives, to live in harmony with our fellow man and the eternal mechanism of the cosmos.

Directions

Fort Rock Ranger District, 1230 N.E. 3rd St., Bend, OR 97701; (503) 388-5664.

Source Notes

Dawson, Maynard C. *Treasures of the Oregon Country*, Salem: Dee Publishing Co. Inc., 1973.

Hagen, Robert D. *Totally Oregon*, Salem: Oregon Pride Productions, 1989.

Multnomah Falls
D. J. Conway

Multnomah Falls is one of many waterfalls in northern Oregon that empty into the Columbia River. What may be the greatest concentration of high waterfalls in North America can be found on the south wall of the Columbia Gorge, the deep chasm through which the mighty Columbia River runs. Eleven falls, all more than 100 feet (30 m) high, can be seen from the freeway or the scenic highway.

The Columbia River drains an area nearly as large as Texas, and it carries the second largest volume of water in the United States (after the Mississippi). It is the largest river in the Western Hemisphere to enter the Pacific Ocean; it is also the seventh longest river in the United States. From the highway, through the Gorge, three snowcapped mountains can

Multnomah Falls.   *Photo by Dennis Graf.*

be seen: Mount Adams (to the north, in Washington), Mount Hood (to the south, in Oregon), and Mount St. Helens (to the northwest, in Washington). Thirty million years of geological history are visible in the walls of the Columbia Gorge, the result of lava flows, erosion and the uplift that created the Cascade Range. Layers of basalt and sandstone can be seen everywhere. The most famous of the waterfalls along the Columbia is Multnomah Falls; it is the fourth highest in the U.S. The main, upper portion of the falls drops sheer down 542 feet (181 m), while the lower falls drops another sixty-nine feet (23 m).

It is possible to climb to the very top of the falls by a trail, but it can be very slick and dangerous because of the mist that rises from the falls and covers the ground. Larch Mount Trail #441 starts on the left-hand side of the lodge at the base of the falls and ascends steeply from the lower falls to the very top. At the one-mile marker, a side trail heads to a viewpoint directly over Multnomah Falls.

Mystical Significance

An ancient, local Indian legend is connected with this beautiful waterfall. A very long time ago, the Multnomah Indians lived in the gorge near a very high cliff along the mighty Columbia River. They were a happy people, living close to the land and in tune with the Great Spirit. There came a time when a terrible sickness fell upon them. Hundreds of Indians died in the epidemic, and no one knew of a cure for the sickness. An old medicine man prayed to the Great Spirit for an answer, tenaciously fasting until he had a vision. The solution that came to him was a drastic one, but the old man called the people together and related his vision. The only way to stop the sickness, the medicine man told them, was for a pure, innocent maiden to sacrifice herself willingly from the sheer cliff. For a time, there were no volunteers, and the sickness raged on. But the chief's daughter sorrowed for her people. Finally, she climbed to the top of the huge cliff and, with prayers to the Great Spirit, threw herself onto the rocks below. The sickness left. In memory of her self-sacrifice for the good and life of her people, the Great Spirit caused the silvery falls to drop from the site of her descent.

Directions

Multnomah Falls can be reached either by the U.S. Scenic Highway Route or directly from I-84, the main freeway through the Columbia Gorge. The Scenic Route begins near the Sandy River at Troutdale, just outside and west of Portland, and ends five miles (8 km) west of Bonneville Dam. Sightseers can enter or exit from either end of the Scenic Route.

Source Notes

Plumb, Gregory Alan. *A Waterfall Lover's Guide to the Pacific Northwest*, Seattle, WA: The Mountaineers, 1989.

Wizard Island
Anodea Judith and Richard Ely

Crater Lake, located in southwestern Oregon, was created 6,850 years ago by the collapse of a huge volcano named Mount Mazama. The lake sits in a cliff-walled bowl five to six miles across, elevated thousands of feet above the surrounding countryside. Crater Lake is the seventh deepest lake in the world. Its shores are surrounded by steep cliffs that are undeveloped except for a single trail that reaches the lake on the north side. The lake is fed almost entirely by precipitation, receiving only a minor percentage from run off from the surrounding cliffs. As a result, very few dissolved nutrients reach the lake, and it contains perhaps the purest natural water known on Earth. Visibility is reported to exceed 130 feet (44 m), and algae has been found growing deeper than 600 feet (200 m)—deeper than anywhere else on Earth. Viewed from the rim, its color is bluer than the sky, ranging from royal blue to indigo to turquoise on sunny days, shimmering silver and gold under the clouds. Close to the shore, the water is so transparent, it is nearly invisible at shallow depths. But where the submerged cliffs plunge downward, the color is a potent violet-blue.

Water in any form is said to be a conduit for the psychic realms. Water has been associated with healing powers, emotional fulfillment, pleasure and cleansing. Water in the form of lakes has a depth we cannot reach, and yet reflects the Heavens in shining glory. In ancient times, priestesses would scry in water to see visions of the future or of scenes far away. In this aspect, Crater Lake can also be seen as a huge scrying bowl of clarity.

Crater Lake was once the site of a large volcanic mountain named Mount Mazama. This mountain began growing about 400,000 years ago atop a 6,000-foot-high (2,000 m) volcanic plateau built of overlapping low, wide basaltic volcanoes (basalt is a dark, very fluid lava such as that making up the Hawaiian Islands). Mount Mazama was actually a compound landform made from a series of smaller, overlapping cones of a more viscous lava called *andesite*. Each cone was active for a time before the eruptions moved elsewhere. The result was a glaciated peak that towered 12,000 feet (4,000 m) above sea level, similar to the other high volcanic peaks of the Cascade Range such as Mount Rainier and Mount Hood.

Approximately 7,000 years ago, the magma beneath Mount Mazama was concentrated in a large, relatively shallow chamber about three to six miles below the base of the mountain. Then, a series of huge eruptions of ash and highly viscous *rhyodacitic* lava removed two or three cubic miles of magma from the chamber and produced such features as Llao Rock, a great cliff that overlooks the north end of the lake. Removal of such a large volume of lava from the magma chamber weakened and fractured the overlying rock, allowing the creation of much larger conduits to the surface. What followed was an eruption that dwarfed the 1980 eruption of Mount St. Helens, releasing a total of twelve cubic miles of magma, most of which was converted to frothy volcanic ash and pumice.

The climactic eruption, which took place about 6,850 years ago, occurred in two stages. The first stage lasted a few days or weeks, resulting in the removal of about five cubic miles of magma from the chamber below the mountain. The second stage of the climactic eruption, which lasted a few days at most, began when Mount Mazama could no longer support itself because so much magma had been removed from below. A huge circular system of faults formed, and the mountain sank into the partially empty magma chamber like a gigantic piston.

Another seven cubic miles of magma roared through the ring of faults, mostly in the form of voluminous, glowing avalanches of white-hot ash that spread up to thirty-five miles (56 km) across the surrounding countryside. In the end, an area of about 5,000 square miles (12,950 sq. km) had been covered with ash to a depth of six inches or more, with about 1 million square miles receiving a millimeter or more. The former site of Mount Mazama was now a caldera, a steaming circular pit about 4,000 feet (1,200 m) deep and five to six miles (9 km) across.

The mountain was quiet now, with only the hiss of steam venting from the hot ash to break the silence. Centuries of rainfall cooled the ash fields, and slowly the great pit filled with water to the level where evaporation and leakage through the caldera wall balanced the inflow. Most of the inflow came from rain and snow, although some came as hot springs rising from the slowly cooling magma chamber. This process probably took hundreds of years, because only the excess of inflow over evaporation and leakage was available to raise the water level. Before the water rose to its present maximum depth of 1,932 feet (600 m), several minor eruptions occurred that built volcanic cones upon the caldera floor. The most prominent cone is Wizard Island, which rises 760 feet (230 m) above the lake surface and a total of 2,250 feet (675 m) above the caldera floor. Its red and black lava cinders and pointed top beckon mysteriously from each and every view of the lake.

Mystical Significance

Not long ago, Crater Lake lay within the lands of the Klamath tribe, a people who had dwelt there for so long that their legends accurately described the eruption and collapse of Mount Mazama. When the Europeans arrived in the area, the Klamath people considered Crater Lake to be a place of such great magical potency that only experienced shamans dared approach it. A number of Klamath legends about the lake are compiled in *Indian Legends of the Pacific Northwest* by Ella Clark (University of California Press, Berkeley and Los Angeles, 1969).

The myth concerning the origin of the lake recounts the attempt of the Chief of the World Below, who lived inside a great mountain where the lake now lies, to secure a bride from the Klamath people. On one of his visits to the Earth, the Chief saw Loha, the beloved of her tribe. He offered her love, eternal life and freedom from sorrow if she would come and live with him. She rebuffed him, and the wise men of the tribe told her to hide herself from him. The Chief of the World Below swore to destroy the people with the Curse of Fire, and raged forth from his doorway at the summit of the mountain. The Chief of the World Above saw what was happening and descended to the summit of Mount Shasta to intercede in behalf of the Klamath people.

A great battle ensued, eventually involving all the spirits of Earth and Air, with oceans of fire and red-hot rocks erupting from the mouth of the Chief of the World Below. The surrounding countryside was consumed in fire, and the tribe fled to find refuge in Klamath Lake. There they held council, and their two greatest medicine men told them that the Curse of Fire had been sent as a punishment for the wickedness of the tribe. Only a willing sacrifice would turn away the wrath of the Chief of the World Below.

Because there were no other volunteers, the two medicine men offered to go, as their years were many. That night they climbed the mountain and jumped into the fiery pit. With that, the Chief of the World Below retreated to his home and the mountain fell in upon him. Torrential rains fell and filled the huge hole where the mountain had been, and the Curse of

Fire was lifted. From that time on, the word was passed from generation to generation of the horrible things that had happened there, and few dared approach that terrible place.

An interesting aspect of this myth is the association of Mount Shasta with the World Above. Today, Shasta is considered one of the supreme New Age holy places in North America, attracting numerous seekers of airy astral realms, the Great White Brotherhood, extraterrestrials and such. Crater Lake is the spiritual complement to Mount Shasta, providing a superb location for descent into the dark, watery mysteries of the Mother Goddess. In the end, both ascent and descent must be experienced by seekers of spiritual wholeness, for those who would walk the path of balance need to be grounded in the sacred Earth as well as open to the heavens.

Another legend told of a lake that was bluer than the sky, with a little mountain island that rose from near its center. The little mountain was the home of the Spirit Chief who ruled over the Land of the Dead. The waters of the lake filled a gigantic cave that led deep into the interior of the Earth. Long ago, the ancestors of the tribe had emerged from inside the Earth, carried up by the flame and smoke that came from the top of the little mountain. Upon death, the spirits of the Klamath people returned to the lake, with the evil ones being confined to the fire pit at the top of the little mountain. The spirits of those who led good lives were free to roam the lake and the surrounding countryside. The Spirit Chief made a law that, under penalty of death, only the wise elders of the tribe might approach his realm to learn from him and consult the spirits of the ancestors.

Directions

Assuming that you are a respected elder in your tribe, Wizard Island can be approached by boat during the central ten weeks of the summer season (dates vary from year to year). You can catch an hourly boat at the base of the Cleetwood Trail, located on the north side of the rim, for $10. The boat ride alone is spectacular, and takes you on a roundabout tour of the special sites not visible from the rim, complete with a geological lecture from a park ranger that is quite informative. (Dress warmly—it's windy out there.) Llao Rock, truncated glacial valleys, and a close-up view of the Phantom Ship (a fascinating rock formation rising up out of the lake) are just a few of the sights visible from the boat. Wizard Island is a stop on the boat tour—if you catch the earliest boat you can stay on the island the rest of the day before catching the last afternoon pickup. The complete boat ride (without getting out) takes almost two hours. No overnights are allowed at this time on Wizard Island—heads are counted!

Once on Wizard Island, you can walk on prepared trails across a field of jagged, broken-up lava called "aa" (pronounced ah-ah). Since the island is relatively young, you can witness an early Crater Lake stage in the process of soil formation, with growing plants and trees appearing in the deep crevices in the lava, which helps to hold moisture and further break up the lava.

There are two main trails on Wizard Island, and you are urged to use the graded ones, as traveling across the "aa" flows is very rough going, and walking across the ash leaves footprints that last for years. One path leads to the western side of the island, where in warm weather, there is a lovely shallow bay suitable for swimming. (The water at any time of year is very cold, however.) There is also a winding trail to the top of Wizard Island, passing through a mature coniferous forest, which leads to the summit crater for which Crater Lake is named—a 300-foot-diameter (100 m) circular depression left by the final eruption of Wizard Island volcano. Wildlife exists on the island, mostly in the form of birds and golden mantled ground squirrels, which were believed to have come across the ice during one of the colder years. (The lake last froze over in 1949.) From the rim of the crater of Wizard Island, you can see all of Crater Lake. The trail reaches the summit on the west side of the crater. As an entrance to an Underworld gateway, this is an apt location, as the sun sets ("dies") in the west, and this direction is mythologically associated with the land of the dead.

The other three cardinal directions are marked by natural features on the crater rim. The eastern side of the rim is graced by a large black lava boulder, which stretches prominently up in altarlike fashion toward the Heavens. The eastern side offers the best view of the lake, as the island is off-center to the western side. A large stand of ghostly dead pine trees, bleached pure white by the elements, occupies the northern part of the crater, further enhancing the lower-world qualities of the place. The highest point on the crater rim is located on the south side. The center of the crater is marked by a large flat surface of black lava (where a small group could gather), with a great flat-topped lava rock at one side. The lowest point of the crater is not at the center, however, but slightly west of center. Numerous loose boulders choke the bottom of the pit, concealing the heart of the old volcanic vent.

Saskatchewan

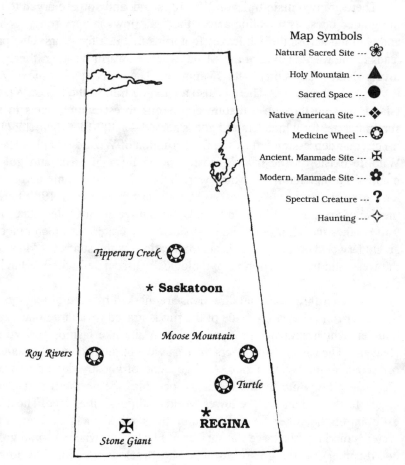

Map Symbols

Natural Sacred Site --- ❀

Holy Mountain --- ▲

Sacred Space --- ●

Native American Site --- ❖

Medicine Wheel --- ❂

Ancient, Manmade Site --- ✠

Modern, Manmade Site --- ❁

Spectral Creature --- ?

Haunting --- ◈

Tipperary Creek ❂

★ **Saskatoon**

Moose Mountain

Roy Rivers ❂

❂ *Turtle*

★ **REGINA**

✠

Stone Giant

The Medicine Wheels
Frank Joseph

One of the most intriguing mysteries in the world is beginning to yield its secrets to modern researchers. But the more they learn, the deeper the mystery becomes. For every question answered, a new one takes it place. This evolving enigma concerns the so-called medicine wheels distributed throughout the western plains of North America. "Medicine" refers to great healing or spiritual power. A typical medicine wheel is a large, circular arrangement of stones marked by crude piles or cairns, and connected by additional lines or "spokes" of stones radiating out from a central rock pile. Although venerated today by various Indian tribes, no historic Native Americans claimed to have built them. Folk traditions in both the United States and Canada assert that the structures were laid out by a pre-Indian people of sun-worshippers. Indeed, modern dating techniques affirm their profound antiquity: an example at Majorville, in Alberta, is 4,500 years old.

In all, fifty medicine wheels are known, most of them clustered along the plains and foothills of the Rocky Mountains from Colorado, Wyoming, Montana and North Dakota, and into Alberta and Saskatchewan. There are at least thirty medicine wheels in Canada. Today, most of them are as removed from population or agricultural areas as they were when they were made on mountain tops or in deep valleys.

In recent years, with the development of archaeo-astronomy, the medicine wheels have unveiled their true function as amazing observatories. They coordinated lunar, solar and stellar information for prehistoric astronomers. The cairns and spokes were precisely aligned to mark solstices sunrises and sunsets, phases of the moon and the appearance of the stars Aldebaran in the Constellation Taurus, Rigel in Orion and Sirius in Canis Major. Typically, a medicine wheel has twenty-eight spokes, which correspond to the number of days in a lunar cycle. Rigel rises just after dawn twenty-eight days after Aldebaran, as Sirius does after Rigel. The surprising sophistication of these and other celestial alignments was powerfully enhanced when investigators discovered that many (if not most or all) of the medicine wheels spread out over many hundreds of miles were originally aligned with each other. More intriguing still, the stony observatories are all radically out of place. One would assume that their function was to act as agricultural calendars to assist farmers in proper planting and harvesting. They should have additionally served as *ritual* calendars for the timely staging of important ceremonies, marriages, business deals and travels, just as the calendars of the Aztecs and Mayas did. But, with a lone exception, there were no population centers of any kind within great distances of the medicine wheels, which are located in barren, sometimes virtually inaccessible territories. Who could have built them in such unlikely areas, and why?

The sky orientations between Wyoming's Bighorn medicine wheel and its counterpart at Saskatchewan's Moose Mountain are exact. The Canadian site is atop the highest hill in the area, seven miles (12 km) north of the town of Kisbey, near Moose Mountain Provincial Park. Its central cairn of rounded boulders is thirty feet (10 m) across. From this center radiate five lines of smaller, rounded rocks forming circles six feet (2 m) in diameter. An ellipse sixty-two feet by fifty feet (21 m by 17 m) encircles the central cairn. Moose Mountain's is the second largest of all the medicine wheels, out-sized only by Alberta's example at Majorville.

Another Saskatchewan wheel may be found south of Rosetown. Twenty-four feet (8 m) across, its circle has an opening to the east, but all its delicate astronomical orientations were spoiled when too many of the most important stones were moved. The Roy Rivers medicine wheel sits on the northern rim of the South Saskatchewan River Valley, just inside the border with Alberta, due east of Empress, on a privately owned farm. Although it too, has suffered some disturbance to its alignments, the summer solstice still sets over Roy Rivers' central cairn, appropriately configured to resemble a sunburst. The Tipperary Creek medicine wheel is unique, because it alone lies among a cluster of other prehistoric sites, fifteen in all. However, archaeologists believe the wheel predates the other remains by many centuries. It rests in a small valley on the bank of the South Saskatchewan River, north of Saskatoon. Twenty feet (6.7 m) across, it is encircled by an outer stone ring of fifty feet and guarded by a trio of spaced cairns.

Among the most provocative medicine wheels is the so-called "turtle" of Minton, high atop a knoll over-looking the Big Muddy River Valley in south-central Saskatchewan, just west of the town. Spanning 130 feet (43 m) in length, a center concentration of stones arranged in a circle has a diameter of thirty feet (10 m), with another "sunburst" configuration at its left side. The "turtle" is actually a *dog*, as proved by the inclusion of ears, testicles, and other distinctly canine, nonreptilian features. It is the only biomorphic medicine wheel, but its bizarre significance lies in the structure's primary axis to the rising of Sirius. Observation of its heliacal appearance was likewise regarded as the beginning of the New Year by the ancient Egyptians, who knew Sirius as the dog star. The Minton structure is not the only parallel with archaeo-astronomical achievements overseas. Aldebaran, which was marked by the medicine wheels, was one of the chief stars used to align Egypt's Great Pyramid.

Not only do the North American medicine wheels and the stone circles of the British Isles physically resemble each other and share often identical celestial alignments; they were also built at the same time. While an ancient astronomer was standing before Canada's medicine wheel at Majorville, watching the sun cast the first shadow of the winter solstice from a stone aligned to mark the event, his contemporary on Britain's Salisbury Plain was doing the same thing at Stonehenge. Hesiod, a historian of Classical Greece, wrote of an Age of Gold that preceded the Heroic Age of Homer's Trojan War heroes. The "gold" Hesiod described was not the glittering metal of wealth, but the gold of the sun, which men worshiped then. They were great astronomers and seafarers, who established an *ecumene,* or world-wide civilization before the Great Flood that destroyed all. This mythic account is reminiscent of Native American accounts, which identified pre-Indian sun-worshippers as the true builders of the medicine wheels. Between these two traditions and among the lonely stone circles of two continents may lie the hidden history of Ancient America.

Mystical Significance

The great mythographer Joseph Campbell wrote that "medicine wheels in the Canadian Rockies can have had nothing whatsoever to do with practical economics: more likely, they reflect what I should call mystical economics, which is to say, the delicate problem of keeping a human community in accord with the rhythmic order of the universe. The proper and primary function of such observatories as those here represented was based on an intuition which underlies all of the so-called 'nature religions' (as distinguished from the monotheistic 'historical religions'), namely, of accord—in depth—with the mystery of the order of nature as the first means and the last end of well being."

The goal of that accord was not only to live in harmony with the natural rhythms of this life, but to proceed successfully into the next. Societies which long and continuously observed the recurring patterns of nature, evolved religious beliefs which reflected their observations. The sun, which always appeared to die in winter returned in spring. The eternity of all life through death to rebirth was a cycle that included human beings. The medicine wheels not only showed them how to follow that cycle while in the material plain, but beyond to the celestial paths of the world beyond.

The surviving medicine wheels of the U.S. and Canada all possess an aura of eternity about them. The circular patterns of their layouts mimics the overhead round dances of the heavenly bodies. Their profound antiquity contrasts with their seemingly modern function as observatories and astronomical computers of surprising sophistication. The remoteness of their locations among the secluded places of nature proves they were set aside as sacred centers of the first order. After an incredible 4,000 years or more, they continue to function just as their mysterious builders intended. The human input of their devotions and the ritual activities of their followers for unguessed generations imprinted the very landscape, the stones themselves with lingering energies made all the more powerful over the course of time.

The medicine wheels still speak to visitors. Those willing to listen may learn the chief lesson these enduring structures were intended to convey; namely, that natural laws are divine laws, and any society which closely follows such laws, as observed in the rhythms and patterns of the heavens, must necessarily draw closer to the gods.

Information

Curator, Archaeology Dept., Museum of Natural History, Wascana Park, Regina, Saskatchewan S4P 3V7; tel. (306) 787-2815.

Source Notes

Campbell, Joseph. *Historical Atlas of World Mythology,* New York: Harper & Row, Publishers, 1988, p. 222.

The Stone Giant
Frank Joseph

"Now giants were upon the Earth in those days." So reads the Old Testament (Genesis 6:4) of a time long before the Great Flood. But the giants did not vanish without a trace. Their enduring images may still be found on remote hillsides or barren plains in Britain, the United States and Canada. These are the colossal geoglyphs of titanic figures carved into the landscape thousands of years ago by unknown artists for a lost civilization. The lone Saskatchewan example is neither the world's largest nor the most perfectly preserved, but it is sufficiently gigantic and impressive enough to generate a sense of awe in the beholder. The effigy is no more than a simple, anthropomorphic outline of boulders portraying a nude male figure with up-raised arms and the suggestion of what may have once been a headgear of some kind.

Laid out in a field near Cabin Lake, in the southwestern section of the Province, the giant measures less than five feet (1.7 m) across at his widest point and is eighteen feet (6 m) in overall length. Depicted penis and testicles leave no doubt to the figure's sexual identity. Curiously, what appears to be a simulated "life-line" extends from the image's throat into the chest cavity to a heart-shaped stone. Local Indians were unaware of its existence prior to its discovery in the late nineteenth century. Consequently, there are no Native traditions to explain the effigy's significance or origins. Also, an undetermined number of its stones have been removed or disturbed, spoiling the original condition of the art work. It has no known astronomical orientations and no population centers occurred in its vicinity, so its ritual function eludes archaeologists. The Cabin Lake giant has only two other counterparts. The nearest is 1,200 airline-miles (1,931 km) away in the California desert, north of the town of Blythe. There, sprawls the ninety-four-foot (32 m) intaglio of a nude male figure, uncertainly dated to the tenth century A.D. The age of the Saskatchewan anthropomorph is even more questionable.

Its other counterpart is much farther away, on a hillside north of Dorchester, England. The Cerne-Abbas Giant wields a club in one hand, while a lion's skin (obliterated over time) formerly draped from his other arm. Here too, dates of origin are dubious, although he was doubtlessly-

143

intended to represent the Greek demi-god, Heracles. (The same mytho-logical character was known 1,000 years earlier as the Phoenician Mel-kart.) Due to some damage suffered at the limbs of the Canadian man-effigy, investigators are not able to determine if it, like the Cerne-Ab-bas Giant, was ever portrayed holding anything. Some researchers specu-late that it depicts Atlas, the titan of Atlantis, because both the stone figure and the mythical king were conceived as virile giants up-raising their arms to support the sky. Is the Saskatchewan effigy the out-sized emblem of Atlanteans in Canada?

At any rate, the three, widely separated examples all portray giants, with emphasis on the genitals. And while they are each stylistically differ-ent from one another, they share too many details to admit mere cultural coincidence. Were they created by the world-wide civilizers of the ancient *ecumene* the Greeks recalled? And is Saskatchewan's stone giant material evidence that they visited Canada?

Mystical Significance

The so-called "box outline human figure" of Cabin Lake, despite its ruinous condition that has rendered the effigy more crude than it appeared originally, has a real sense of presence. Visitors feel the simple power intended in the giant by his creators, unknown centuries ago. Primary emphasis is on the up-raised hands (what *were* they supporting, if any-thing?), the prominent genitals and the heart with its curious life-line. The figure's mythic symbolism is apparent, but indecipherable. What does it mean? The geoglyph's size implies power; its supportive gesture, strength; its heart, life itself; its prominent penis, virility, fertility. These are qualities that supplicants appealed for from the rulers of heaven. Looking down on them from the sky, the gods were supposed to see the symbolic effigy and get the message.

Beyond these cultic speculations, the Stone Giant, without the need to intellectually grasp its details, speaks directly to our inner-knowing. We are profoundly impressed, without understanding exactly why. The uni-versal symbol by-passes our rational brain to address something forgotten but not obliterated in us. It stirs in us less than a half-memory of a greatness long past, that was once ours. By allowing the figure to speak to us in his own way, if we are only patient and open-minded enough, we will hear his voice telling us things we half-remember, yet long to know.

Directions

From Swift Current, take Highway 32 to Cabri. Follow the signs to "Man Effigy," fifteen minutes from downtown.

Information

Saskatoon Visitor & Convention Bureau for directions assistance: 310 Idywyld Dr. N, Box-369, Saskatoon, SK S7K 3L3; tel. (306) 242-1206.

Tourism Saskatchewan, 122 3rd Ave. N, Saskatoon, SK; tel. (306) 664-6240. Open week days 9:00 A.M. to 5:30 P.M.

Source Notes

Indian Boulder Effigies, Saskatchewan Museum of Natural History Popular Series, Nr. 12, Regina, 1965.

Utah

Map Symbols

Natural Sacred Site ---

Holy Mountain --- ▲

Sacred Space --- ⬤

Native American Site --- ❖

Medicine Wheel --- ⊛

Ancient, Manmade Site --- ⊞

Modern, Manmade Site --- ✿

Spectral Creature --- **?**

Haunting --- ◈

★ SALT LATE CITY

Canyonlands

Zion National Park

Hovenweep ✿

Zion National Park
L. Christine Hayes

The book, *Zion National Park: Towers of Stone,* by J. L. Crawford, tells us the park's name was bestowed in an enlightened moment by a Mormon settler named Isaac Behunin: "One evening while sitting on his front porch in the lingering twilight, he gazed across the vast expanse of the canyon. He was so moved by its grandeur that it inspired him to remember a passage in the Bible (Isaiah 2:2), which mentions a place called Zion, found 'in the top of the mountains,' where 'the Lord's house shall be established.' Isaac felt that he had discovered such a place, and from that moment on, he called it Zion."

This national park in southwestern Utah contains high cliffs, mesas and deep canyons of extraordinary beauty. The major portion of the park was established in 1919; it was expanded in 1956. In all, it occupies an area of 229 square miles (594 sq. km). Since Utah is largely a Mormon (Church of Jesus Christ of Latter Day Saints) state, the unique geological features of the park are named after the historical-religious beliefs of the Latter Day Saints. Some of these sites include: the East Temple, Towers of the Virgin, Temple of Sinawava, Mount Moroni, Angels Landing, Mountain of the Sun, the Beehives, the Three Patriarchs and the Great White Throne (an awe-inspiring visage of stone rising 2,394 feet [798 m] above the canyon floor). Winding through the impressive vistas of the park is the Virgin River.

Zion is abundant in wildlife, harboring and nurturing such animals as mountain lions, mule deer and more than 150 species of birds, including hawks and eagles. Although this is a semi-arid region, broad-leaved trees and wildflowers grow near the river. The Anasazi (a Navaho word meaning ancient ones) Indians once inhabited this land, living in small villages containing large circular, semisubterranean "pit houses." It would seem that they abandoned the Zion region by A.D. 1200, somewhat earlier than did their brethren in other areas of the southwest. It is believed that they eventually became part of the ancestors of the Hopi Indians.

Mystical Significance

The area of Zion National Park was, and continues to be, held sacred by Native Americans. When visiting Zion years ago, I was told of the distress Native Americans of the region feel in seeing so many people camping in the park. To them, it is a sacred temple, a place to pray, meditate and talk to the gods and ancestors. They do not like to see people playing, eating and sleeping there, anymore than we would wish to see people camping in the Cathedral of St. John the Divine. But the park is not only sacred to Native Americans. I have seen cities of interdimensional forms residing within the natural crystalline towers of the park. Reverence is the key of entry to the Temple Zion. Enter it as you would a church. You are most definitely not only on sacred ground, but within a Holy House.

A message was channeled by this author on May 30, 1990. (Channeling is the offering of one's mind and voice as vehicles of communication for an other-dimensional being who imparts teaching or guidance through its human contact.) The following information on the park was given:

> From the summits of Earth's majesty, sacred places on high, doth the energy of the Light Tower's (holy entities of planetary consciousness once incarnate as leaders on Earth) bonding to this orb abide. As these mounts of matter shed their hulls, they become Knights ridding the steeliness of their armor for the robes of quest. They shine forth the rays of the Light Towers, calling them to the bosom once again, being caught upon the winds, like birds of flight. Numbering among these dwelling places of SHEKHINAH are Mount Sinai (Sinai), Mount Tabor (Israel), Ayers Rock (Australia), the man-made, star-designed Pyramid of Giza (Egypt) and also Tor Hill (Glastonbury, England), whose etheric body dwarfs the 'hill' of matter in which the greater form resides.

> As these energies are released...so they penetrate the *Door of Zion*, which is the Perfected Nation, the Absolute Realm that suffers no bondage to those who behold its golden chains, links to the Kingdom within. In the world of matter, this Door is to be found most prominently in the sacred land of Zion National Park, in Utah. This place between land and (etheric) sea contains the greatest aggregation of consciousness for the New World matrix. She is a silent angel, whose trumpet gleams in the moonlight, awaiting a rising sun. She walks unshod among men, her face hidden from them. No pilgrimages are made to her granite tresses, no sepulchers of anointing are raised within her folded wings. Yet her horn will surely issue a clarion call with the dawning of a Day soon to rise above the shoulders of the world. Only those who Guardian her breaches know the kindling flame within. It is within her body that the Light Towers survive their antiquity to become vigorous servants whispering through the cacophony of endless dreams, those seed-thoughts of new visions for the Children of Zion.

The meaning of this message is that there is a conductive energy that is contained in certain sacred high places, such as Mount Sinai, and even the man-made Pyramid of Giza. This special energy penetrates the Door of Zion, which is both a spiritual state and a physical place. The physical place is that of Zion National Park, which is called a "silent angel," for it is not a well-known spiritual center as is Mount Shasta (California) or Sedona (Arizona). Zion National Park is a collection of spiritual energy containing holy tones or signals for future spirit-matter creation. Upon the threshold of the New World, we will need to be brought into unison with other dimensions of reality that bridge our own, connecting us to Spirit. The crystalline structure in Zion contains the engrams or programs for this evolution of our realm into a greater absorption of spirit being. Divine commands were imprinted in nature's hand long before we descended as into the Eden consciousness to begin our plight as star-born beggars at the temple gates. Zion is the last and the first of these Temple gates. It is the last of the Old World and the first of the new.

Directions

Take Interstate 15 from St. George, Utah, to Hwy 9, which will take you through the small towns of Hurricane and Virgin, and on into Zion National Park.

Information

Zion National Park map, published by the National Park Service in Utah.

Source Notes

Crawford, J. L. *Zion National Park—Towers of Stone*, Sequoia Communications, p.46. This book can be purchased from the Zion Natural History Association, Zion National Park, Springdale, UT 84767. To order by phone: 1-800-635-3959 (credit cards only).

Temple Doors, issue #2-90, published by the Star of Isis Foundation, PO Box 4872, San Antonio, TX 78285.

Hovenweep
Florence L. McClain

Hovenweep (Deserted Valley) is a Ute name given to six groups of ruins in southeastern Utah and southwestern Colorado. Square Tower, Horseshoe, Holly, Hackberry, Cutthroat Castle and Cajon are unique even in this land of the unusual. Long, lonely canyons cut through almost barren mesas, offering little promise of an environment compatible with human life. But each canyon guards a secret—a life-supporting spring of water. Surrounding the approaches to these springs, majestic stone towers cling to the canyon rims or rise from the tops of solitary boulders, over mounds of brush-covered rubble that was once pueblos, giving silent testimony that human beings once lived and thrived in this harsh land. The builders of Hovenweep were bold and innovative, adapting their designs to the peculiarities of the terrain. That they were intelligent and observant is evidenced by reservoirs and check dams built on the mesas above the springs, which caught the runoff from the sparse rainfall and

Hovenweep Boulder House, Utah.   *Photo by Florence L. McClain.*

allowed it to percolate through the strata, enhancing the flow of the springs. They terraced the lower areas of the canyons and raised crops of beans, squash and corn.

The monument headquarters is located at Square Tower Group. Here, as at the other ruin groups, self-guided trails meander up and down the canyons to allow visitors to examine these architectural wonders. Whether it is Hovenweep Castle or Stronghold House at the Square Tower Group, or Tilted Tower at Holly, or Cutthroat Castle or any of the other strange and beautiful ruins, you can only respect and marvel at the ingenuity and skill of the craftsmen. (Actually, many archaeologists and anthropologists say that women were the builders of the southwest U.S.)

As harsh and stark as the land appears at first sight, there is great beauty in the settings. A blue, blue sky serves as a fitting background for the golden-red sandstone. Patches of bright green pinpoint springs and seeps. And on the eastern horizon, seeming an appropriate memorial to the ancient peoples who once labored here, is the reclining figure of a man: Ute Mountain, commonly called "The Sleeping Ute."

Hovenweep, Utah.   Photo by Florence L. McClain.

Mystical Significance

Whether for mystical or purely practical reasons, or a combination of the two, the people of Hovenweep were observers of the skies. Square Tower Group, Hovenweep Castle and Unit-Type House give evidence of this. The doorway and small windows of the large D-shaped tower of Hovenweep Castle appear to mark the summer and winter solstices and the spring and autumn equinoxes at sunset on those days. At Unit-Type House, four small openings mark the solstices and equinoxes, and possibly the nineteen-year cycle of the moon.

At Holly Group, under a rock ledge just south of the Great House ruin, is an astronomical device reminiscent of the Sun Dagger at Fajada Butte in Chaco Canyon, New Mexico. Three figures are pecked on the wall of a narrow sandstone passage. On the left are two spirals. One appears to have been partly obliterated by either water seepage or erosion. A short distance to the right, the classic Pueblo sun symbol is represented by three concentric circles with a dot in the center. Faintly visible just to the left and below the sun symbol are two small circles joined by a line—a twin figure which may represent the Morning Star and Evening Star, twins of Pueblo mythology. To the right of the twin figure is the figure of a snake.

On the morning of the summer solstice, approximately an hour after sunrise, an arrow of light appears to the left of the spirals. As it crosses the second spiral, a second arrow of light appears to the right of the sun symbol and begins to move across it until the tips of the arrows join into one band of light. This process occurs over a period of about seven minutes. The band of light then moves down the sandstone wall until the twin figure and the bottom section of the snake are illuminated. This device also notes the spring and fall equinoxes, but the winter sun at the time of the solstice does not reach the spirals on the sandstone wall. Possibly there are other solar observatories at Hovenweep that have disappeared as buildings fell into ruin.

Perhaps the most mystical aspect of Hovenweep is that human beings came into what appears to be a hostile environment and were able to flourish and live in harmony with the environment. They did not come with the attitude of "conquer and subdue." This is seen in the fact that they did not attempt to change the terrain to accommodate their buildings, but adjusted their buildings to the existent terrain. They were not content to simply use the life-giving springs. They did what they had learned through observation to aid nature in conserving water and giving life to the springs which made their lives there possible.

Directions

From Cortez, Colorado, take US 666 northwest to Pleasant View, then at the sign, take the unnumbered county road twenty miles (32 km) west. Or, from Blanding, Utah, take Highway 191 south to Highway 262. Turn east to Hatch Trading Post. From there, follow the dirt road sixteen miles (26 km) to Square Tower Monument Headquarters. Maps to other ruin groups are available there. The roads leading into Hovenweep are graded dirt, and can quickly become muddy and impassable during and following rainstorms. At best, the roads are rough and a high-clearance four-wheel-drive vehicle is preferable.

Canyonlands
Florence L. McClain

Canyonlands. Unique lands. Mysterious, grotesque, beautiful beyond reality—the leavings of heaving Earth, surging waters, eroding winds and rain, and time—vast eons of time.

Each mile unfolds a changing vista. Mountains still snow-stippled in early summer; wildflower meadows that bloom in the spring and again after late summer rains; undulating waves of slickrock that look as if sandy beaches and ocean waves have been frozen into stone; deep, lonely canyons that bombard the senses with feral beauty around each turn; eerie mazes of sandstone spires eroded into fantastic shapes that fire the imagination; and soaring arches that frame skies of incredible blue. The Anasazi have left equally intriguing traces of their long ago presence. Sharp eyes can see tiny granaries or cliff dwellings tucked into seemingly inaccessible niches high on sheer cliffs. Ruins of stone houses dot the perimeters of meadows where crops once grew. Exotic, spectral figures painted or pecked on canyon walls evoke a profusion of emotions as you wonder what inspired the artists. One red, white and blue figure, remarkably prescient of the United States flag, is aptly named The All-American Man.

Other rock art portrays familiar creatures—deer, rabbits and bighorn sheep. One particularly touching record is almost lost among a host of figures pecked on a rock wall. Large footprints are accompanied by much smaller footprints ending at the body of a deer pierced by an arrow. One can almost see the proud father making a record of the first hunting trip with his young son. There are also rows of red hand prints with strange lines etched in the palms.

In the heart of this fantasyland, a trail begins on the bank of a usually dry wash. The primitive path crosses Chesler wash and leads up among the strangely eroded columns of sandstone. Not heavily traveled, it twists and turns, not always easily discerned as it crosses rocky outcrops. Occasional wildflowers are in bloom, seeming exceptionally beautiful because of their scarcity. A few cacti have found pockets of soil to sustain life. Stunted junipers and pinon pines provide infrequent bits of welcome shade. (The pinon pines are commonly found in the southern Rocky Mountain region and notable for the large seeds they bear.) Off the trail, areas of sandy soil are covered by a black crust called cryptogamic soil. (It is vital to plant life that this crust remain undisturbed and intact. It protects the soil from erosion and helps to hold what little moisture this area receives. A careless footstep can destroy it for many years, perhaps permanently.)

One tree, long dead and turned silvery gray by sun, rain and time, stands twisted and coiled into a work of art lovely enough to grace any museum. After almost a mile, the path leads to a narrow stair of stacked rocks. Climbing up, you enter a passageway that is dark and cool. This is the entrance to "The Joints." A short distance ahead, a large boulder and a smaller, flat slab of rock are flooded with light in the center of a junction open to the sky. A few yards to the right, an opening leads outside. To

Canyonlands, Utah.   *Photo by L'Aura Colan.*

the left, around the boulder, the path enters a narrow crack, or joint, between high, sheer walls of stone. The pathway is covered with several inches of white sand. For almost a mile you are in a strange world of stone and sand roofed by a narrow band of indescribable blue. Occasional side joints branch off, most leading to dead ends or narrowing to impassable cracks. At times the walls narrow so that both can be touched simultaneously. It is quiet and tranquil and has a strange, intense beauty.

At one point, a tumble of boulders seems to choke the narrow passage. These can be easily climbed to the path that continues at a slightly higher level. At the end, a stone stairway leads up and out into the broad basin of Chesler Park. Rolling waves of rock, creased by narrow, seemingly bottomless fissures, are bordered by soaring cathedrals and spires of red sandstone banded with white. In every direction, either nearby or on the far horizon, there are feasts for the eye.

Mystical Significance

This red land holds danger for the imprudent, i.e., the careless or inexperienced off-road driver, the ill-prepared backpacker, the foolhardy and overconfident and those who ignore or choose to be ignorant of the perils of the terrain. A sudden rainstorm upstream can turn a dry creek bed into a raging torrent within minutes. A canyon floor may seem to offer a firm crossing when it is really a trap of quicksand just beneath the surface.

Paradoxically, this is a benign land, a quiet land, a place of rare tranquility. There are no power lines, no telephones, no highways crowded with vehicles and there is no sky filled with airplanes. The sounds are songs of nature: a gentle breeze, a buzzing insect, an ebullient bird call, the distant, lonely cry of a coyote or there is profound silence.

Somehow, this area of the Canyonlands seems to shed human vibrations as easily as it sheds the sparse rainfall. Events which have occurred throughout the countless centuries have left only physical evidence in the ruins and rock art. The psyche has the rare opportunity for autonomous exploration of self in relationship to the challenges of the surroundings uninfluenced and unhampered by old psychic records of other times and peoples or interference from modern technology. It is seldom, if ever, in our busy world that we have the opportunity to be so completely alone with self. This place is indifferent to human presence. It remains whether we go or stay, live or die. Each individual has the choice of how profound or superficial the experience will be.

The only experience that is unavoidable is the self-knowledge which is gained when you are forced to meet and handle emotional and physical challenges presented by the environment. The challenge of simply getting there and returning can be formidable.

Directions

Getting into the Needles district of the Canyonlands requires a great deal more than just knowing which road to follow. The roads are minimally maintained and can quickly become impassable for several days during rainstorms. The road surface varies from deep, sandy ruts to washboard and rock ledges and steep slickrock grades. A high-clearance four-wheel-drive vehicle with an experienced driver is a necessity. It is preferable that at least two vehicles travel together. Carry equipment and tools for emergency repairs. A pair of hand-held CB radios is a good investment. Over some of the steep areas of rock ledges, the driver has poor visibility of the roadbed. Someone walking ahead to direct the driver can prevent serious damage to the vehicles. Chances are that you may not see another vehicle or person while you are in the interior of the Canyonlands. Assume that you are essentially on your own and plan for it.

Water is of primary importance. Water is limited, usually nonexistent and the dry desert can cause rapid dehydration. Drink frequently enough to satisfy your thirst and then a little more. Carry at least one gallon of water per person per day for drinking and extra for other needs. Carry extra food and water for emergencies.

Campgrounds are primitive. Be prepared to sleep in your vehicle, in the open or in a tent. There are no sanitation facilities. All trash, including toilet paper, must be carried out. Burnable trash may be burned if you have a campfire in a designated site. All firewood must be brought in from outside the park and all ashes must be carried out.

Good maps of the area and the ability to use them are essential. The roads and trails may not always be exactly as shown on the maps. In some instances, roads and trails outside the park boundaries may no longer exist. Do not judge travel time by the mileage involved. If no side trails other than The Joints and Chesler Park are explored, allow one-day travel time to get into the area of Bobby Jo Camp from Dugout Ranch (approximately forty to forty-five miles), one day for exploration of The Joints and Chesler Park, and one day for exiting by way of the SOB Hill—Elephant Hill Route (approximately twelve miles [20 km]).

Take Highway 191-163 north from Monticello, Utah, fourteen miles (22 km) to Highway 211 across from Church Rock. Turn west on 211. At approximately ten miles (16 km), stop for a look at Newspaper Rock State Park, then continue for approximately eight miles (13 km) to the Dugout Ranch turnoff on the left. Here, you will be leaving the paved road and turning onto a dirt road that is very rough and needs high clearance in some areas. It will climb out of Cottonwood Creek onto Bridger Jack Mesa, then cross Salt Creek Mesa. Continue to follow the road into the Beef Basin area through House Park, Middle Park and Ruin Park into Pappy's Pasture. Somewhere in this area you may see a sign: County Maintenance Ends. You are allowed to laugh, cry or make whatever remarks seem appropriate. At this point, the road becomes a primitive jeep trail and descends a steep grade of sand, loose rock and rock ledges into Bobby's Hole. Stop at the top of the grade and explore the condition of the road before committing yourself to it. Many people consider this segment of road as one way—down only. When it is dry, others do choose to come out this way rather than going out by Elephant Hill. Do use extreme caution in either direction.

At the bottom of this grade, ignore the sign (if it is still there) which says: "Abandon hope, all ye who have entered here," and continue on for approximately six or seven miles (about 10 km) until you see a sign on the left for Bobby Jo Camp and Horsehoof Arch Camp. You will probably be more than ready to make camp. From Bobby Jo Camp, it is approximately one mile (1.6 km) to the spur on the right that leads to The Joints-Chesler Park trailhead. This mile is rough in places, and at least one area has very tight clearance for tall vehicles and campertops. It is a half mile (0.8 km) on the spur to the trailhead, where you may park. There is one picnic table and an outdoor toilet, but no water.

You may choose to return by the same route if the condition of the climb out of Bobby's Hole permits. Otherwise, return to the main trail from The Joints-Chesler Park spur and turn right (north) into Devil's Lane. This is one of many "grabens"—long, narrow, rock-walled valleys. The first obstacle to be tackled is called SOB Hill. The name is well earned. Rock ledges, loose sand and rocks, tight turns and generally rough road make it memorable. At one point a very tight turn ascending a rocky ledge is impossible to make with a frontal assault. You will note an area you can head into which then makes it possible to back up this segment. A large vehicle will have a great deal of difficulty with this maneuver. Approximately three miles from the Joint-Chesler Park spur, on the far-side of SOB Hill, a trail turns to the right toward the Devil's Kitchen Camp. **Do not** make this turn. It is part of a one-way loop to Elephant Hill. Shortly past this spur you will encounter a half-mile segment known as the Silver Stairs. These are relatively smooth rock steps with drops of from three to four feet, so named from the color of the metal left from the undercarriages of passing vehicles. Proceed with caution.

Approximately a mile (1.6 km) beyond the Silver Stairs the trail junctions. Take the junction to the right toward Elephant Hill. You will note the Devil's Kitchen segment of this one-way loop joining the Elephant Hill trail after a little more than two miles (3.5 km). Another mile or so brings you to the base of Elephant Hill. This is the most difficult part of any of the roads you have encountered so far. It is most wise to walk the road and look at the problems involved. It consist of steep rock ledges and narrow switchbacks. Take note that it is necessary to back up one switchback segment and plan accordingly. You will also note that it is necessary to back onto a rock ledge over-hanging the canyon to get in position to make the approach to the final brutal segment to the top. Slow and steady in low-low four-wheel drive guided by an observer with a hand-held CB should bring you safely to the relatively flat mesa, possibly to the cheers of less-daring folk who have parked their cars on the far side and climbed up to watch the fun.

Here you can stop and take a break before attempting the descent from Elephant Hill. The descent is over steep grades of rough, loose rubble and then down a very steep slickrock slope to a graded dirt road. At this point it looks like a super highway. Closely observe the rock wall on the left side of the road between Elephant Hill and the Squaw Flat Campground where the pavement begins for interesting Anasazi rock art. The pavement is Highway 211, on which you can return to Monticello. Do not attempt this exit route without at least four to five hours or more of daylight. You may, if you choose, enter the Needles District of the Canyonlands over the Elephant Hill route. Should you choose to backpack, you can park either at the Squaw Flat Campground (usually full in good weather) or at the base of Elephant Hill. There are backpacking trails from both points, which enter the north side of Chesler Park. They are minimally maintained, not always well marked, and not for the neophyte. You should carry water and food for a minimum of two days.

Another possible approach is from Blanding, Utah. Take Highway 191-163 south to Highway 95, "The Trail of the Ancients." Turn west on 95 for approximately seven miles (11 km) to the first paved road, turning north between Brushy Basin Wash and Cottonwood Wash. Approximately six miles (10 km) north at the junction, go left. The pavement will end shortly after crossing Cottonwood Wash. Twelve miles (19 km) will bring you to Kigalia Ranger Station and the junction to the right, which is known as Elk Ridge Road or the Big Notch Road. Go approximately fifteen miles (25 km) north, where you will join the road coming in from Dugout Ranch, a few miles south of the Beef Basin area.

Inquire about road conditions in Blanding. This road over the Abajo Mountains is very narrow and is covered with snow or deep mud into late spring. Once committed, there is little, if any, opportunity to turn around. It is beautiful country but makes the approach from Dugout Ranch seem tame. It is difficult to be exact about mileage. Signs are sparse to nonexistent. Details may vary from map to map, but maps and a compass are your best tools for a successful trip.

Information

Trails Illustrated Topo Map of Needles District, Canyonlands National Park, Utah. (Highly recommended.)

USGS fifteen-minute series topo maps for The Needles, Fable Valley, Harts Point, and Mount Linnaeus quadrangle.

Quick and excellent service on phone or mail orders from Holman's Inc., 401 Wyoming Blvd, N. E., Albuquerque, NM 07123-1096; tel. (505) 265-7901.

Southeastern Utah road map (highly recommended). Published by Utah Travel Council, Council Hall, Capitol Hill, Salt Lake City, UT 04114. These maps and others are available at area visitor centers.

Source Notes

Barnes, F. A. *Canyon Country Prehistoric Rock Art* (no. 14), Salt Lake City: Wasatch Publishers Inc., 1990.

Barnes, F. A. *Utah Canyon Country* (no. 1), Salt Lake City: Utah Geographic, 1991.

King, Henrietta. *Unknown Utah*, New York: McMurray Publishers Inc., 1972.

Rolf, Michael. *A Guide to Utah's National Parks*, Salt Lake City: Lawrence Review Books Inc., 1980.

Washington

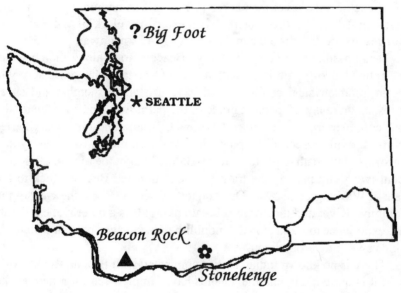

? Big Foot

★ SEATTLE

Beacon Rock

▲

Stonehenge

Map Symbols

Natural Sacred Site --- ✿

Holy Mountain --- ▲

Sacred Space --- ●

Native American Site --- ❖

Medicine Wheel --- ⊙

Ancient, Manmade Site --- ✠

Modern, Manmade Site --- ❀

Spectral Creature --- ?

Haunting --- ✧

Beacon Rock
D. J. Conway

Beacon Rock, the core of an ancient volcano, is a gigantic monolith that juts 850 feet (255 m) above the edge of the Columbia River and is the second largest in the world after Gibraltar. It stands a few miles downstream from Bonneville Dam on the Washington side of the Columbia River. The conical peak itself rises 848 feet (255 m) on a base of only seventeen acres (7 ha). It was named, by Lewis and Clark in 1805, for the fact that it alerted travelers of a clear river journey to the Pacific Ocean 150 miles (242 km) away.

It is possible to hike to the top of Beacon Rock along the chiseled, one-mile (1.6 km) path lined with a maze of metal railings. Be sure you are in good physical condition and have a head for heights and sheer drops, as there is a 15 percent grade to the path. A plaque partway up the trail commemorates the work of Henry J. Biddle and his aide, Charles Johnson, who preserved the pinnacle from becoming a rock quarry and constructed the path to the top. Henry Biddle bought the rock in 1915, and spent two years blazing the trail. His heirs donated Beacon Rock to the state of Washington in 1935. Once on top of Beacon Rock, the view of the Columbia River and the gorge is breathtaking. It is a quiet, yet exhilarating, experience to stand atop the monolith with the ever-present Columbia winds sweeping around you.

There is no known Indian legend connected with Beacon Rock. However, it is quite likely that the legends have simply been forgotten, as the local Indian tribes had myths connected with almost every natural feature in the region. Local tribes called Beacon Rock by the name of "Che-che-op-tin," the Navel of the World.

Mystical Significance

Although none of the Native American traditions surrounding Beacon Rock are believed to have survived the passage of time, that single, very possibly ancient reference to it as the "world navel" is intriguing, because it is a title that occurs throughout the Earth, wherever the practitioners of a high religion established themselves. On the island of Gran Canaria, in the Canary Islands, off the Atlantic coasts of North Africa, the Natives worshipped at a great rock similarly regarded as the navel. On the other side of the planet, tiny Easter Island, in the South Pacific, was aboriginally known as the Te Pito Te Henua, the Navel of the World. The island of Delos, in the eastern Mediterranean, and the Greek Delphi, on the Gulf of Corinth, were both consecrated navels centuries before the time of Alexander the Great. Rome, too, had her *Umbillicus sacra* at the centrally located Temple of Saturn.

A complete list of all such "navels" would include locations in virtually every ancient civilization in both the old and new worlds, including Asia. And everywhere the same, essential elements are found in place with the navel-concept: an oddly shaped mountain or rock used to symbolize a belief in the evolution of the soul through reincarnation. This karma-cult is believed by some researchers to have been the religious impetus behind a world-civilization, an *ecumene* spoken of by the Greeks of the classical age, that long before the Trojan War established the first planet-wide civilization, then perished in a terrible cataclysm of nature. In any case, Beacon Rock's ancient identity as a navel of the world might mean it was once the center of a reincarnation-religion and part of the Earth's first planetary civilization. All that remains of that lost achievement is its name, Che-che-op-tin.

Directions

Beacon Rock State Park can be reached by crossing the toll bridge at Cascade Locks. Turn left on State Route Highway 14 and follow the road for about four miles (6.5 km) west. If traveling east from Vancouver, Washington, follow Highway 14 for approximately thirty-five miles (57 km); the State Park is about eighteen miles (29 km) east of Washougal, Washington. The rock is clearly visible from both sides of the Columbia River.

Source Notes

Drawson, Maynard C. *Treasures of the Oregon Country*, Salem, Ore.: Dee Publishing Co., 1973.

Drews, Paul. *Simulacrum: the Recreation of Sacred Architecture*, New York: Macmillan Inc., 1986.

Lyons, Dianne J. Boulerice. *Washington Handbook*, Chico, Calif.: Moon Publications, 1989.

Sunset Travel Guide to Washington, Menlo Park, Calif.: Lane Publishing Co., 1978.

Vogel, Henry. *Washington, My Washington*, New York: Grosset & Dunlap Inc., 1977.

Stonehenge
D. J. Conway

The impressive replica of world-famous Stonehenge was constructed in 1920 by Samuel Hill. He also built the Maryhill Museum nearby. But his megalithic reproduction in concrete was commemorated to the regional Klickitat County veterans who died in World War I. Since Sam Hill was four decades ahead of the decoding of the original Stonehenge's positions, his model is unfortunately not aligned to any particular direction.

The Washington Stonehenge, as a full-sized, authentic replica of England's ancient site, produces a feeling of awe in those standing within the circle of monoliths. Situated near the edge of the massive cliffs of the Columbia Gorge, Hill's Stonehenge occupies a barren, lonely area, but full of peace and beautiful views. If you cannot visit the original structure in England, this is an excellent place to experience some of the grandeur and awesomeness of a megalithic circle. But because this is a fairly modern site, there is no venerable tradition associated with the place. However, modern Druids have celebrated many rituals at Stonehenge, thus building up a certain amount of energy within it. There appear to be strong currents of both Earth and air energies within the circle.

Mystical Significance

The Principle of Sympathetic Magic, as stated in the *Egyptian Book of the Dead* (circa 1800 B.C.), holds that if a sacred object is faithfully and reverently duplicated, some of the original's spiritual power will be transferred into the replica. A mechanical reproduction will not do the trick. But if high intent is at work, the sacred simulacrum will partake of the first source. This, according to numerous visitors, has been accomplished at Washington's Stonehenge. Indeed, Hill fulfilled the first and most important requirement in creating sympathetic magic, when, long before the concrete was laid, he conceived of it as a monument to his fallen countrymen. His noble intentions comprised every atom of the materials that his sponsorship molded into a duplicate of that premiere sacred site at Britain's Salisbury Plain.

Moreover, the circle is the most ancient and basic unit of a sacred site; so much so, it is the very symbol of a sacred center, imitating as it does the eternal energies of the cosmic soul, so often exemplified in the celestial phenomena once computed by the original Stonehenge. In its Washington counterpart, we see it as it appeared before the Romans dismantled it. The very restoration of so hallowed and spiritually potent a monument must supercharge Hill's achievement with kindred sparks. Doubtless, the Washington Stonehenge is a sacred site, where all things may be possible.

Directions

From Seattle, take I-90 to I-82 at Ellensburg. Head south to 97 at Buena. Follow 97 until it crosses Hwy 14, about 2 miles (3.5 km) east of the Maryhill Museum. Posted signs direct visitors to a right-hand turn onto a narrow, paved road. Another right-hand turn takes them to a short dirt road that meanders across open fields to Stonehenge.

Stonehenge, Washington.   *Illustration by William Wild.*

Yukon and
Northwest
Territories

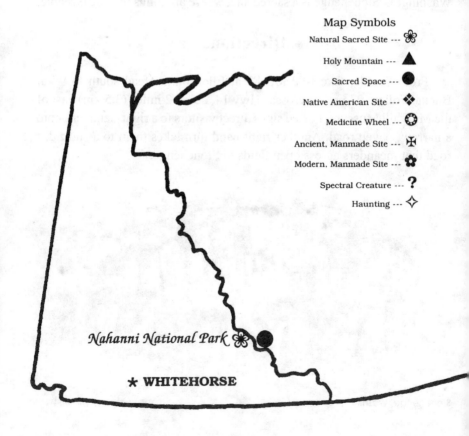

Map Symbols

Natural Sacred Site --- �֍

Holy Mountain --- ▲

Sacred Space --- ●

Native American Site --- ◆

Medicine Wheel --- ☸

Ancient, Manmade Site --- ⌘

Modern, Manmade Site --- ✿

Spectral Creature --- **?**

Haunting --- ◇

Nahanni National Park ✿ ●

✶ **WHITEHORSE**

Nahanni and the Northern Lights
Frank Joseph

Bleak tundra landscapes, impossible cold, caribou herds and a turn-of-the century gold rush. These are the wild, often forbidding images conjured by the name Yukon in the minds of most people who have never visited this part of the world. Although not inaccurate, the stereotype is drastically incomplete and results only from a superficial acquaintance with northern Canada.

The Native peoples, whose ancestral ties with the territory go back an incredible 30,000 or more years, know the secret of the land. But outsiders who come here with the proper mind-set and an open heart may approach the mystery through their own, personal experiences. The secret is this: almost the entire Yukon is a sacred site, certainly one of the most powerful on Earth. An expert geomancer in *feng shui* (a Chinese term for interpreting the spiritual character of a particular landscape) traveling through the Yukon and Northwest Territories would be overwhelmed by the magnitude of their telluric power.

Many outsized and extreme natural elements combine to make the *genius loci* here a force of almost monstrous energy. The coldest Yukon temperature recorded to date was in 1947, at Snag, in the western part of the interior, where the mercury hit -80°F (-62°C). Residents enjoy telling first-time guests that the region has only two seasons: this winter and last winter. Each summer solstice, twilight lingers into sunrise, from which the title, Land of the Midnight Sun, originated. Six months later, on the winter solstice, darkness reigns unbroken by a ray of sunlight for twenty-four hours in northern towns like Old Crow. But these extremes in temperature and solar behavior account for only part of the magical atmosphere.

While great regions comprise stark tundra, boreal forests spread for 175,500 square miles (281,000 sq. km), almost 60 percent of the Yukon. There are white and black spruce, pine, birch, poplar and, in the southeast, tamarack. But the brilliant diversity of the area's flowers is perhaps most surprising for newcomers. More than 1,300 species of wildflowers, ferns and shrubs flourish throughout the territory, making a luminous contrast against the imposing mountains and subarctic climate. Lavender petals of the Yukon crocus break through the snow in early spring. They herald the flourishing return of wild roses, tiny orchids, violets, poppies, columbines and anemones. By midsummer, many forest floors are spread with broad carpets of blue lupins, while meadows of arctic cotton replace winter snows in swampy tundras.

Many world travelers believe Emerald Lake, north of Carcross beside the Klondike Highway, is the most stunning body of water they have seen. Although only about a mile across, deposits of copper on its bottom transform the water into an electric blue-green unmatched elsewhere. Singular locations like Emerald Lake, the sudden annual flowering of life and its equally abrupt disappearance set the mood of enchanting strangeness that pervades the Yukon.

Its largely unspoiled and unpopulated vastness impacts each visitor with vistas of the Earth in the starkness of its original purity. Experiencing the sweep of its mountain and forested landscapes is to behold our planet at a time long before mankind set foot here. Nature is unbowed, unconquered, serenely eternal, unique in all the world for reasons more profoundly felt than readily verbalized. Like hearing the dramatic performance of a Beethoven symphony, we are stirred to the sanctum sanctorum of our souls, but can provide no rationale for our reaction. We can only feel the emotion, not explain it.

The Yukon would be sacred enough for the interplay of its natural extremes and the enormous scope of its primeval solitude. But its numinous power rises to unprecedented heights in that most awesome celestial phenomenon, the Aurora Borealis. At no other place may this heavenly tableau be seen to such spectacular advantage. Great curtains of luminous deep scarlet, purple azure and emerald green descend from the zenith of the night sky, as though we were attending the commencement of some godly theatrical event. It is usually at its most brilliant in March and April and from late August to late October. This apparition results by way of streams of electrically charged particles from the sun traveling together as a "solar wind." Streaming through the North Pole's magnetic field, they fall into our planet's ionosphere some 100 miles (160 km) above the Earth, and their collision releases energy to create the phenomenon. The same effect occurs at the South Pole, where it is known as the Aurora Australis, although the "Southern Lights" are not as bright as their Arctic counterparts, for reasons not yet entirely understood.

Although the Northern Lights are visible all across northern Canada, they take on a special significance at Nahanni National Park, located in the southwest corner of the Northwest Territories, straddling the provincial border with the Yukon. Among the world's premiere parklands, its 1,840 square miles (4,760 km) of virtually pristine natural environment may be reached only by charter aircraft and boat or on foot.

The often savage South Nahanni River frantically dances through 183 miles (295 km) of the imperious Mackenzie Mountains to deluge over Virginia Falls. At 410 feet (137 m) high and 656 feet (219 m) across, they are twice the size of Niagara. Opening at the titanic base of the falls is one of North America's deepest gorges, with canyon walls reaching 4,000 feet (1,334 m).

Nahanni is rich in spiritual focal-points from which to view the Aurora. The huge expanse of its strange, powerful wilderness is the perfect setting for experiencing our planet's most dazzling sky show.

Mystical Significance

Nahanni National Park is among Canada's greatest peculiar sacred sites, with a reputation for high weirdness almost as ancient as its own mountains. Its name originates with a half-spectral Native tribe much feared by the Gwich'in Indians. The Nahanni are spirit-beings who can manifest themselves as powerful flesh-and-blood men in order to guard a lush, tropical valley of balmy breezes hidden somewhere in the Mackenzies. This Shangri-La of the North is inhabited by lovely maidens and lissome boys trapped by the subarctic environment outside. They offer themselves and gold nuggets the size of marbles to anyone able to get past the guards in attempts at persuading visitors to remain with the precocious youngsters forever. A very few outsiders supposedly found a way into the valley, but none have ever returned.

A century ago, Albert Fallie, an otherwise successful prospector, took the legend very seriously and spent his entire life looking for the place. In 1905, three brothers of the McLeod family renewed the quest in earnest. Their whereabouts were unknown until a trio of neatly laid out skeletons was found three years later. Each skeleton was missing a skull. Hence, the name of the stream near their discovery, Headless Creek. Since then, other searchers vanished in their hunt for the elusive Eden, and some have been found murdered under enigmatic circumstances. Modern travelers in Nahanni still pass through Deadman Valley and the Funeral Mountains. But these mysterious incidents of foul play are extremely infrequent, given the more than one hundred years over which they occurred.

Native stories of the valley of the Nahanni may be related to the Aurora Borealis observed and ritually celebrated in what is now a national park. For example, the Eskimos and Tlingit Indians believe the Northern Lights take place after the death of many people, whose souls are at play in the night sky. The Saulteaux say the dead are dancing in the ghostly movements of the Aurora. A variant on their interpretation by the Kwakiutl portrays the lights as the dance of a family's deceased members performing for the living who will soon die. The Gwich'in say the lights are caused by the dead who, taking pity on mortals below, light the long polar night with spectral fires.

This Native Canadian association of the Northern Lights with death is repeated on the other side of the Arctic Circle. Finnish folk tradition likewise describes the phenomenon as the souls of the dead dancing their way toward heaven. The Norse and their Viking poets sang of the Aurora as the light of Valhalla glinting off the shields wielded by the Valkyries, daughters of the gods, as they carried the souls of heroes slain in battle to heaven's resplendent citadel.

Whether the remarkable similarity of these beliefs among peoples distantly separated from each other resulted through prehistoric contact and influence from one group upon another, or was the outcome of their common origins in the deeply remote past, no one is certain. Only the Inuit do not associate death with the Northern Lights. According to them, the Aurora is the visualization of time. A skilled interpreter of natural phenomena, a shaman who comprehends the spiritual underpinnings of all things, may read by the cold, colorful lights descending from heaven everything that has happened or shall be.

Perhaps the otherworldly valley of the Nahanni is that paradise of eternal youth and spring each human being carries around inside his or her soul. It is that still-point of perfect tranquility generated by the powerful harmony of Earth Mother's Nahanni National Park below and around us and Sky Father's appearance in the Aurora Borealis high above.

Directions

From the Yukon capital at Whitehorse, take Highway 1 east to Highway 4. Go north to Highway 10 into Tungsten. From here, the main road leads directly to Nahanni National Park. Be prepared to leave your car and proceed on foot.

Various licensed outfitters offer trips from six to ten days usually beginning at Virginia Falls, then through the canyon via canoes or inflatable rafts. Recommended operators include Nahanni National Park Service, Box 348-EG, Fort Simpson, NT X0E 0N0; tel. (403) 695-3151; Nahanni River Adventures, Box 4869, Whitehorse, YT Y1A 4N6; tel. (403) 668-3180, and Nahanni Wilderness Adventures, Box 4, Site 6, RR# 1, Didsbury, AB T0M 0W0; tel. (403) 637-3843.

Information

Superintendent, Nahanni National Park, Postal Bag 300, Fort Simpson, NT, X0E 0N0; tel. (403) 695-3151.

Source Notes

Tempelman-Kluit, Anne. *Discover Canada: Yukon*, Toronto: Grolier Limited, 1994.

Fodor's Canada, New York: Random House, 1996.

Lightbody, Mark and Tom Smallman. *Canada, a Travel Survival Kit*, London: Lonely Planet Publications, 1992, p. 703.

Frommer's Canada, New York: Macmillan Co., 1996.

Leach, Maria, Editor. *Funk & Wagnall's Standard Dictionary of Folklore, Mythology and Legend*, New York: Harper & Row, 1972, p. 91.

Epilogue

The sacred sites described in the preceding pages await visitors in search of a personal quest to the Otherworld. And that, in effect, is what all these bizarre places share in common: they are gateways from our material level of existence into the spirit realm, the Kingdom beyond time. The reasons for going through such a mysterious gateway are varied and may range from the need for physical or psychic healing to an inner craving for spiritual fulfillment—to have one's soul touched by something greater than ones's self, yet kindred.

Whatever the compulsion, seeking out these magical centers must inevitably reestablish that profoundly mystical link between our deepest inner being and the living planet. They are places of joyful reunion for the Earth Mother and us, her children. Certainly, such homecomings are the best reasons for visiting any sacred site.

These locations will "work" for us if they are accepted as gifts. And we must know how to be gracious in the acceptance of such gifts. It is our attitude alone—not any inherent magic at a particular site—that determines the validity and personal significance of our visit. Sacred sites close themselves off to the ignorant and the insincere, the mean-spirited and cynical. But the centers are also wonderfully giving of themselves to anyone who approaches them conscious of the holy ground on which he or she stands.

Guardians of the sacred site open its doors to the honest pilgrim only. Sacred sites are landmarks on our own quest through the world. They are sign posts along the hero's journey toward the authentic life.

Frank Joseph,
January 1997

MORE GREAT HANCOCK HOUSE TITLES

History

Barkerville
Lorraine Harris
ISBN 0-88839-152-8

B.C.'s Own Railroad
Lorraine Harris
ISBN 0-88839-125-0

Cariboo Gold Rush Story
Donald Waite
ISBN 0-88839-202-8

The Craigmont Story
Murphy Shewchuk
ISBN 0-88839-980-4

Curse of Gold
Elizabeth Hawkins
ISBN 0-88839-281-8

Early History of Port Moody
Dorothea M. Norton
ISBN 0-88839-197-8

End of Custer
Dale T. Schoenberger
ISBN 0-88839-288-5

Fishing in B.C.
Forester & Forester
ISBN 0-919654-43-6

Fraser Canyon Highway
Lorraine Harris
ISBN 0-88839-182-X

Fraser Canyon Story
Donald E. Waite
ISBN 0-88839-204-4

Fraser Valley Story
Donald E. Waite
ISBN 0-88839-203-6

Gold Creeks & Ghost Towns
N. L. (Bill) Barlee
ISBN 0-88839-988-X

Gold! Gold!
Joseph Petralia
ISBN 0-88839-118-8

Living with Logs
Donovan Clemson
ISBN 0-919654-44-4

Lost Mines & Historic Treasures
N. L. (Bill) Barlee
ISBN 0-88839-992-8

The Mackenzie Yesterday
Alfred P. Aquilina
ISBN 0-88839-083-1

Pioneering Aviation of the West
Lloyd M. Bungey
ISBN 0-88839-271-0

Vancouver Recalled
Derek Pethick
ISBN 0-919654-09-6

Yukon Places & Names
R. Coutts
ISBN 0-88826-082-2

MORE GREAT HANCOCK HOUSE TITLES

Native Titles

Ah Mo
Tren J. Griffin
ISBN 0-88839-244-3

American Indian Pottery
Sharon Wirt
ISBN 0-88839-134-X

Argillite: Art of the Haida
Drew & Wilson
ISBN 0-88839-037-8

Art of the Totem
Marius Barbeau
ISBN 0-88839-168-4

Coast Salish
Reg Ashwell
ISBN 0-88839-009-2

End of Custer
Dale T. Schoenberger
ISBN 0-88839-288-5

Eskimo Life Yesterday
Hancock House
ISBN 0-919654-73-8

Guide to Indian Quillworking
Christy Ann Hensler
ISBN 0-88839-214-1

Haida: Their Art & Culture
Leslie Drew
ISBN 0-88839-132-3

Hunter Series
R. Stephen Irwin, MD,
Illustrations J. B. Clemens:

Hunters of the Buffalo
ISBN 0-88839-176-5

Hunters of the E. Forest
ISBN 0-88839-178-1

Hunters of the Ice
ISBN 0-88839-179-X

Hunters of the N. Forest
ISBN 0-88839-175-7

Hunters of the Sea
ISBN 0-88839-177-3

Images: Stone: B.C.
Wilson Duff
ISBN 0-295-95421-3

Indian Herbs
Dr. Raymond Stark
ISBN 0-88839-077-7

Indian Tribes of the NW
Reg Ashwell
ISBN 0-919654-53-3

Iroquois: Their Art & Crafts
Carrie A. Lyford
ISBN 0-88839-135-8

Kwakiutl Art & Culture
Reg Ashwell
ISBN 0-88839-325-3

More Ah Mo
Tren J. Griffin
ISBN 0-88839-231-1

My Heart Soars
Chief Dan George
ISBN 0-88839-231-1